Emotional Victory

How *to* Deal *with* How You Feel

Bud Calvert

Author of the Book God's Passion

First published in 2012 by Striving Together Publications, a ministry of Lancaster Baptist Church, Lancaster, CA 93535. Striving Together Publications is committed to providing tried, trusted, and proven books that will further equip local churches to carry out the Great Commission. Your comments and suggestions are valued.

Striving Together Publications
4020 E. Lancaster Blvd.
Lancaster, CA 93535
800.201.7748

Cover design by Andrew Jones
Layout by Craig Parker
Edited by Ted Wieler and Tina Butterfield
Special thanks to our proofreaders

The author and publication team have given every effort to give proper credit to quotes and thoughts that are not original with the author. It is not our intent to claim originality with any quote or thought that could not readily be tied to an original source.

ISBN 978-1-59894-195-1

Printed in the United States of America

DEDICATION

The great joy of my ministry was the privilege of starting and pastoring the dear people of the Fairfax Baptist Temple for thirty-five years. It was a responsibility and an accountability that I never took lightly. With the joy of pastoring God's people in this church body came the necessity from time to time to help some hurting sheep get back on the path of righteousness.

Life is not always the proverbial "bed of roses." We often find briars and barbs along the way that have a tendency to interfere with God's will for our lives. Thank you, dear FBT family, for allowing me the privilege of not only learning with you, but also helping you along life's journey. It is to you that I dedicate this book.

Table of Contents

ACKNOWLEDGMENTS

My sincere thanks to a fellow staff member and attorney at FBT, Dr. Ted Wieler, for his careful and insightful editing of this book.

Thank you to my wife Mary for always supporting and encouraging me, as well as helping with the book.

My special thanks goes to Dr. Paul Chappell and the publishing arm of Lancaster Baptist Church, *Striving Together*. The wonderful staff there, under the leadership of Cary Schmidt, has always been most gracious and helpful.

Introduction

What is your expectation of the day when you first open your eyes in the morning? I doubt that your first conscious thought is something like "I feel as though God is going to abandon me." Quite the contrary, I think most of us are relatively optimistic early in the morning. Our thoughts are "Today is going to be a good day" or "I plan to get a lot done today." It is our nature to be happy and confident.

However, it is also our experience that our days do not always unfold the way we had planned. Maybe you've stepped in the shower to find there is no hot water. Then you soon find that hot water has flooded the basement. Or perhaps you've pulled onto the highway with plenty of time to get to work when BAM! Suddenly you are locked between two other cars. The one in front of you slammed on its brakes, and the one behind you thought that a following distance of eight inches would be enough space to react.

Happily, for the most part, we are resilient and able to accommodate the seemingly endless number of unexpected side steps we are required to take as we continue down life's path. But often the events of a day come upon us without warning, and they take control of our lives. Things happen to us that we do not anticipate, and in our frustration, thinking ourselves innocent, we turn our eyes heavenward and ask, "God, where are You?" "God, why did You let this happen to me?" Even those without a personal relationship with Jesus Christ find fleeting thoughts about God having abandoned them. After the surprise of the thought departs, those who have a personal relationship with Christ are often quick to whisper a prayer asking God to forgive them for doubting His promise that He will never leave us nor forsake us.

First Peter 5:7 says, "*Casting all your care upon him; for he careth for you.*" The quality of God's care is explained a little more completely in Psalms 55:22 which says, "*Cast thy burden upon the Lord, and he shall sustain thee: he shall never suffer the righteous to be moved.*" God will "sustain" or maintain—guide, make provision for—those that turn to Him. The verse also states that God will not allow the "righteous to be moved"—to slip, shake or fall into decay. God promises to preserve those who call out to Him. It is the active presence of God's Spirit ministering to our spirit that allows Christians to "keep the faith" and experience emotional victory through life's tumultuous difficulties.

For some, the weight of life's events becomes increasingly difficult to carry. Those who do not know Jesus Christ personally have no one to cast their burdens upon. And many who *do* know Christ, unexplainably do not cast their burdens upon the Lord. The result is a person who is so encumbered that they experience negative reactions physically, emotionally, and spiritually. For those so affected, it is proper to say that they are in crisis—a place of instability. For the person at a crisis point—at the moment that they are perhaps least capable—a critical question must be answered that will shape their future: "How will I deal with how I feel?" Even through the hardest of times God's Spirit desires to give you emotional stability and victory.

This book began as a series of sermons originally preached from the pulpit of Fairfax Baptist Temple. We will look at thirteen different burdens or cares that are commonly experienced. As a pastor for thirty-five years and someone who has dedicated himself to learning the Bible for even longer, these issues of life have been common to me. Our Saviour writes in Hebrews 4:15, *"For we have not an high priest which cannot be touched with the feeling of our infirmities; but was in all points tempted like as* ***we are, yet*** *without sin."* Being a preacher is not a shield from the cares, difficulties, or anxieties of life. I have been burdened by some of the things I have written about to the point of tears. What might have separated me as a pastor from those that I had been charged to lead is the amount of time I allowed myself to carry these events before casting them onto my Saviour.

It is my testimony that I do not waste much time or energy trying to find my own way out of the maze of life's distractions. I understand these events to be temptations that could turn me from complete fidelity to my God, and I claim 1 Corinthians 10:13 saying, *"There hath no temptation taken you but such as is common to man: but God is faithful, who will not suffer you to be tempted above that ye are able; but will with the temptation also make a way to escape, that ye may be able to bear it."*

The purpose of this book is to explain from the Word of God how to escape the temptation of sin when facing life's hurdles. It is my hope that you will find in these pages reassurance or reason to have peace and joy even in the midst of trials. For those who are saved, this book may serve as a reminder. For those who do not have a personal relationship with the Creator of the universe, this book is an invitation to that relationship, for it is the first step toward a fulfilling life and an eternity where there will be no memory of the struggles that may presently cause you to tremble.

I

When You Feel God Is Not Interested

MARK 4:35–41

And the same day, when the even was come, he saith unto them, Let us pass over unto the other side. And when they had sent away the multitude, they took him even as he was in the ship. And there were also with him other little ships. And there arose a great storm of wind, and the waves beat into the ship, so that it was now full. And he was in the hinder part of the ship, asleep on a pillow: and they awake him, and say unto him, Master, carest thou not that we perish? And he arose, and rebuked the wind, and said unto the sea, Peace, be still. And the wind ceased, and there was a great calm. And he said unto them, Why are ye so fearful? how is it that ye have no faith? And they feared exceedingly, and said one to another, What manner of man is this, that even the wind and the sea obey him?

I'm sure that all of us have, at some time or another, felt as if we were shipwrecked on a desolate little island, battered by an ocean full of troubles and abandoned by everyone—including God. Most of us consider ourselves good people, and therefore, we resort to wondering why bad things should happen to us. During times of adversity we are tempted to question: "Why me, God? Have You no feelings for my pain? Is there not some value to my life? Do You really care?"

Along with the pain of difficult circumstances, we often experience dejection, as Jeremiah did when he lamented, "*My strength and my hope is perished from the LORD*" (Lamentations 3:18). He was so forlorn that he thought, "All hope is lost. Not even God cares. With nothing to look forward to, I cannot even muster the strength to go on."

Are you there, friend? Does it seem that God has forsaken you? Mark 4:35–41 relates a story about Jesus' disciples feeling that way. From this story, we can take heart; even when it seems that God is indifferent to our difficulties, even when He seems far away, His watchful eye sees. His wise hand directs. His tender heart cares.

A Glimpse into the Life of Jesus

As the sun crept steadily westward, the crowd gathering along Galilee's shore continued to swell. Some came to see a miracle. Others came hungry to hear from this wise teacher whose simple parables created an appetite for the truth. All of them felt drawn to this man who was unlike anyone they had ever before encountered.

The crowd grew to a great multitude, making it difficult for all to see and hear. Concerned for these yearning souls, Jesus directed His disciples to launch a humble fishing vessel away from the shore. From this vantage point, He preached passionately, His message resonating across the water's gentle ripples until the sun's glowing rays finally touched the horizon. With the day long spent, Jesus asked His disciples to send the multitude away, and when the last stragglers were gone, the Master devoted the day's final moments to expounding the truth of the parables to His chosen twelve. The last hint of golden light dissipated, and the Lord, weary from a long day of teaching and preaching, said to them, *"Let us pass over to the other side."* With that, they weighed anchor and began their trip across the Sea of Galilee.

As the shore behind them grew distant, the disciples, with full hearts, reflected on the events they had left behind. It had been thrilling to see crowds gather in droves to listen to their Master's powerful words. How privileged they had felt as Jesus plainly expounded the truth to them once they were alone. Now that they were away from the crowds and the demands of a taxing season of ministry, they looked forward to a little relaxation and some fellowship with their Lord. They all needed a little rest.

But this placid scene ended abruptly when gusts of powerful wind blew in suddenly from nowhere. As the wind grew more ferocious, it hefted up walls of water and dumped them mercilessly on the vessel, which pitched and reeled in the turbulent sea as if it were a child's toy. Everyone manned his post, working desperately to gain control of the situation. Some of the men were rowing with the oars to steady the boat. Others were bailing with buckets. Everyone was working hard—everyone, that is, except Jesus. The storm came upon them so unexpectedly that, at first, no one seemed to notice Jesus was missing.

Before long, even the seasoned fishermen among them began to panic. Barring a miracle, the ship would surely sink, and they would all die. When they finally realized that their circumstances were impossible, they thought to look for Jesus.

I imagine that the disciples were appalled when they found Him in the back part of the boat, lying down on a pillow fast asleep, for they cried to Him through the tumult, *"Master, carest thou not that we perish?"*

I wonder what ran through their minds. Perhaps in their desperation some thought, "Why are You sleeping while a storm is raging? We're about to lose our lives! Don't You care what happens to us?" I can hear others thinking, "We've been following Jesus, and look what it has gotten us—trouble!" I imagine someone else saying, "Never again will I see my precious children!" I believe that, at this point, with a storm raging all around them and hundreds of feet of water underneath them, all the disciples thought it had been a bad decision to follow Jesus when He said, "Let's go to the other side."

Calming the Storms of Life

What did Jesus do in response to their fears and worries? He rose from the paltry rest He had been allowed. His beloved disciples were in trouble. They needed His help. With composed dignity, Jesus straightened Himself to rebuke the roaring wind and calm the turbulent waters. "All right, wind, that's enough. And, sea, peace, be still." At His command, the howling gale immediately died to a soft, pleasant breeze, and the hammering waves to a sheet of glass. One moment they were being pummeled brutally; the next moment they might have been on a pleasant excursion. The contrast was so eerie that it struck awe in their hearts. The disciples looked at each other and asked, "*What manner of man is this, that even the wind and the sea obey him?*"

The Lord turned to them and said, "*Why are ye so fearful? How is it that ye have no faith?*" (Mark 4:40). In essence He was saying, "Hey, you guys have a problem. When in the world are you going to learn that you can trust Me, even in the midst of dire circumstances?" Can you hear Jesus talking to His disciples in the now calm ship? "I said we would go to the other side of the lake, but look at you; you're all upset and panicked. Why should you lack faith when I am right here with you?"

Just as the disciples lacked faith during their storm, we also experience lapses and lose sight of the fact that the Lord is with us, and just as they accused Jesus of indifference to their plight, we also charge God with apathy. Very often we echo the sentiments of the psalmist who cried, "*Why standest thou afar off, O Lord? why hidest thou thyself in times of trouble?*" (Psalm 10:1). Certainly, at these times we think, "If there is a God in Heaven who cares, He would look down, and deliver me from my problems, and calm the storm I'm feeling."

God is always working all things for our good, and although seemingly bad things happen to us, it isn't because God is not good. On the contrary, He knows exactly what we need to mold us and shape us into the person He wants us to become—the very image of Christ. We have much to learn during this process of transformation, and God can use hardships to teach us. In fact, hardship is one of His most effective teaching tools.

As a thirteen-year-old, while riding my bike one day down a hill, I accidentally stuck one of my fingers in the spokes! Back in those days we used to have sirens on the front fork of our bikes that would have a chain attached to it. We could pull the chain and the siren would rub against the wheel and generate an authentic sounding siren (which is why they eventually banned them). Well, my chain was broken. So while going down a hill and picking up speed, I reached down without looking to grab the siren and pull it up against the tire. However, I missed the siren and stuck my hand into the spokes, and I went flying! I got home and walked into the house nonchalantly, but when my sister noticed my injury, she screamed, "Look at your hand!" I looked down at the broken finger, which stuck out about ninety degrees from the others, and realized I couldn't move it. Of course, my sister felt it her duty to run and tell our mother, who rushed me to the hospital emergency room.

The doctor told me, "Because you've just eaten, I can't give you anything to make you unconscious" (I think it was ether they gave back when I was a teenager). "You can spend the night here, and tomorrow morning when your stomach is empty, I can put you under and snap your finger back in place, or I can go ahead and do in right now without any anesthetic."

I thought, "It's just going to be a little snap that will hurt for a moment." So I said, "Fine."

He wrapped his hand around that finger. It was just for a minute or two, but it seemed like an hour or two. Finally he finished, and I thought, "Wow! That was painful!" I must have commented because the doctor said, "Oh, I haven't done it yet. I was just finding where the bone is." At that point, I began to have second thoughts, but it was too late. He took that finger and yanked it back. You talk about hitting the ceiling! I was not a happy camper when the doctor was finished with my torture.

Fixing my finger hurt like nothing else I have ever felt, but the finger feels fine now. It hurt in order to help. Sometimes when trials come into our lives, we struggle to deal with the pain, and we wonder, "Doesn't God care?" But every hurt has a purpose in our lives.

Although it may be difficult to do, we must hang on to the ship during the storm, believing that God is not going to let it sink. When we come through the storm, it is important that we ask, "What can I learn from this?"

By the way, sometimes people have the idea that storms come to their lives because they have disobeyed God or because God is against them or because God is uninterested. For the believer, it is never true that God is uninterested or unconcerned. And, it is not always true that storms are the result of disobedience, although some are. Jonah ended up in a storm because of his disobedience. He ran from God and His will, but that is not true of Jesus' disciples in this story. I'd like to point out that they ended up in a storm precisely because they chose to obey.

Hey! These disciples weren't living in sin! They were living good lives—such as you would expect of Sunday school teachers and preachers. They were sharing the Word of God. They were supporting the Lord Jesus Christ as He preached to multitudes of people. They were in the will of God, exactly where God wanted them and doing exactly what God wanted them to do, but the storm came. And storms will come into your life as well.

Dealing with the Storms of Life

I came up with a little acronym that forms the word *storms* to help us understand the storms that we can expect to come our way. Keep in mind that our loving, wise God uses the storms of life to make us more mature, more like Christ.

STRESS

The first "S" in *storms* comes from the word *stress.* Stress may be due to external or internal sources. Face it, there are thousands of little things that we have to cope with every day.

I have lived in the Washington, D.C. area almost my entire life, and during these many years, I have never heard any of the thousands of people who have transferred here say that they are looking forward to the slow pace of Washington, D.C. But I do hear these new people say, "This is stress city! Why would anyone come to Washington?" Some are almost in tears as they lament, "What have I done wrong? I thought this was a promotion, not a demotion!" Life in this area is very hectic.

But regardless of the place we call home, we can all make our lives stressful with the unreasonable ambitions or expectations that we impose upon ourselves. We get our eyes on the value system of this world and believe that we need to achieve a certain rank or perform to some undefined level or have just a few more possessions if we are to measure up in this world. These self-imposed goals, in turn, cause secondary stress on the job or in our family relationships, and a vicious cycle of stress dominates our lives.

TRIALS

The "T" is *trials.* These are the circumstances that are beyond our control, the things that we didn't expect to happen, the events that catch us by surprise.

With trials come heartaches, and with heartaches come questions: "God, why did this happen to me?" In the middle of a storm, good Christian people may look around at the seemingly calm life of the ungodly and wonder, "Why, Lord? I know some wicked, ungodly heathens who have better lives than this. It just doesn't seem fair."

We start questioning God, demanding to know why He allowed this storm in our lives. "It doesn't seem fair that he got the promotion, and I didn't." "It doesn't seem fair that she is getting married, and I'm not." These kinds of questions will focus your attention on the wrong person: you!

Remember the story in Matthew 14:22–31 of Jesus walking on the water? Peter, impetuous Peter, tested our Lord saying, *"if it be thou, bid me come unto thee on the water."*

Jesus said, "Fine, Peter, come on out." Peter climbed over the side of the boat and started walking toward Jesus. *"But when he saw the wind boisterous, he was afraid; and beginning to sink, he cried, saying, Lord, save me"* (Matthew 14:30). Peter turned his attention from Jesus and focused on himself and his powerlessness against the storm swirling about him. When he let his thoughts, and probably his eyes, turn from Jesus, he began to sink.

Peter's self-focus was the root cause of his difficulty. Still, we can learn something valuable from this impetuous disciple. Notice his response. He did not cry out, "Lord, why did You let this storm come into my life?" Consider how irrelevant that question would have been at that point. When one is about to slip beneath the waves, it is of little value to know God's reason for the storm. Whatever the reason, our response must be the same as Peter's when he found himself overwhelmed by the storm, *"Lord, save me."* Our focus should return to the One who can truly help.

When we find ourselves questioning, what we are really seeking is deliverance. We want God to remove the storm so that our lives return to calm and rest, but peaceful seas do not develop a crackerjack sailor. It is weathering the storms that makes him a capable seaman.

Demanding of God that He make known the reason for a particular storm, especially while we are in the middle of it, is one of the greatest weapons Satan employs to weaken our faith. We must be careful during trials to keep our focus on the Lord.

OTHERS

The "O" is *others.* We all have people problems from time to time. These problems are usually the most painful, producing a gamut of emotions such as anger and self-pity, even deep bitterness. People problems may manifest themselves on the job, even to the point of altering the direction of a person's life as he moves from job to job to escape workplace conflict. The most ravaging effects occur in homes and churches as the devil has a heyday pitting people one against another—husbands against wives, children against parents, and Christians against Christians.

In all of these situations, it is tempting to isolate ourselves from further pain or confrontation. We may think, "Well, if that's the way he is going to be, I'll just avoid him." "Why, if that's the way that church is, I don't need those people." With no peace, we have to face an often cruel world without the encouragement of those God put in our lives to bless us.

Mark it down, you'll never resolve problems by avoiding them. The way you handle problems is confronting them head on and going right through them. The process may hurt; it may be messy, but that's the way you get help. I had to endure a little pain to get my broken finger fixed, but a few moments of pain brought about the healing that I needed.

REASONING

The "R" is *reasoning.* There is just something about us that makes us want to solve our own problems. We want to prove that we are capable of handling any situation, but sometimes we come up against a situation that simply eludes our reasoning. When life has spun out of our control, we often become bitter and conclude that God is unjust in allowing such affliction or adversity to come our way. This kind of human reasoning is nothing more than deciding our way is right and God's way is wrong. Consider how ludicrous it is that we finite, frail, human beings should think ourselves wiser than an infinite, all-knowing God.

There is a bigger lesson to learn here. Sure, there are some circumstances in life that we can manage, but the self-sufficient and arrogant attitude mentioned above is one reason so many people choose a false path to salvation instead of the Bible way. We think, "Look what I've done. I finished school. I got this degree. I got that job. I got this promotion. I can accomplish what I put my mind to." But when it comes to determining where we will spend eternity, self-effort is useless. The Bible tells us salvation is by the grace of God alone, not by the works we do.

The fact that we can do nothing to earn our own way to Heaven defies human reasoning. It seems logical that our good deeds must outweigh our bad if we will be deemed worthy to go to Heaven. That's why the majority of religions teach that a man must do something to attain acceptance from God. The problem with that kind of reasoning is that it contradicts the teaching of the Bible. God's Word says, "*there is none that doeth good, no, not one*" (Romans 3:12b). "*There is none righteous, no, not one*" (Romans 3:10). No matter how hard man tries, he will never stand righteous before a holy God. No amount of self-effort will ever *earn* a place in Heaven. There is no possible way for an unrighteous man to gain acceptance with God, except by placing his faith in the Lord Jesus Christ.

The Bible likens salvation to the birth of a baby. A great deal of pain and labor are involved, but it is not the baby who does the work. He is carried along as a result of his mother's efforts. Likewise, if we will be born into God's family, we will be carried along as a result of Jesus' suffering on our behalf, for it is His bloodshed and death that paid the price God demands for our sin. When we accept God's Son as our personal Saviour, God accepts us. He deems us righteous because our sin debt is paid in full by the blood of Christ. Each man must come by faith and say, "Lord, nothing to the altar I bring, simply to Thy cross I cling."

The problem is human reasoning says, "That's too easy. We have to *do* something to earn our way." That kind of reasoning will stand in the way of a man humbly trusting Christ as his only hope for Heaven.

MONEY

The "M" is *money.* "Boy," you might say, "if money causes storms in our lives, mine should be smooth sailing because I certainly don't have much!"

That's exactly the storm I'm talking about—financial pressure. There always seems to be too much month left at the end of a paycheck.

In America, we have so much that we feel we are entitled to live by the standard that we deem our prerogative as citizens of this country. A vast segment of society lives in a financial stratum that we consider to be poverty level when, in truth, we don't really know what poverty is. The solution reached by our nation's legislators is that we tax everybody else to subsidize those who they are convinced do not have enough. They believe this transfer of wealth will elevate these folks to a higher level. "God may have forgotten them," they say, "but we are here to help them." This "help" has produced a generation who believes that financial prosperity is their right.

This attitude of entitlement has pervaded our society to the extent that even many Christians have fallen into the trap of believing God to be unfair if He does not provide the things they expect. Have you ever found yourself thinking this way: "Certainly, if God were really interested in my life, He would ease this financial pressure and give me the things I need"?

Sometimes a financial storm is a storm of our own making because of our unreasonable expectations and standards. In any case, financial pressure can be a difficult storm to endure.

SERVICE

The final "S" in *storms* is *service.* Even for those serving God, frustrations arise. You may be busy serving God, helping out around the church, ministering to people, yet feel that you aren't really making a difference. Troubles come and people fail. You may question whether you are truly doing God's perfect, specific will for your life, or you may think, "If what I am doing is so important, God would plainly show me the answer for the problems I am facing." You may be tempted in self-pity to think, "He just must not care about me."

During all these storms, it makes sense that you, like the disciples, should focus on self-preservation. After all, it is *your* ship that's sinking.

You are the one in peril. Anyone can see that it's reasonable for you to look out for yourself. It's reasonable, but it's not necessarily right. After Jesus calmed the wind and the sea, He rebuked His disciples with these words: "*Why are ye so fearful, how is it that ye have no faith?*"

Likewise, when we forget that Jesus is in the ship with us, when we lose sight of Him and put the focus on ourselves, we begin to believe that He is not interested. That lie is exactly what the devil would have us swallow. It is based on feeling, not fact. And a feeling is nothing more than that—a feeling. It is not a barometer for truth or a guide for our decisions or our behaviors. When storms come, we need a Compass to point us to True North. We need the truth found in God's Word.

What Is the Real Truth?

The disciples felt alone in their difficult circumstances, as though Jesus had forsaken them in their time of need, but this belief in Jesus' indifference was completely unfounded. As fear and despair overwhelmed them, they lost sight of a few truths regarding their situation. These are truths we too should consider and cling to when problems come and we feel isolated from God.

1. Jesus promised to go with them to the other side. Keep in mind that it was Jesus' idea that they should cross the Sea of Galilee that day. The disciples were guaranteed safe passage for one simple reason: Jesus would be with them the entire way. This fact would not eliminate their need to use their seafaring skills. In fact, Jesus employed their skills as they set out on this trip. He wanted to show them that they could rely on Him rather than on their own strength. Jesus had said that they would go to the other side, and His presence was enough to ensure that they would arrive at the destination without harm.

As I pointed out earlier, they were in the storm because they were doing what Jesus told them to do. Likewise, when we are obedient to the Word of God, we don't have to fear.

2. The disciples should have realized that nothing is too hard for the Lord. They had already seen Jesus restore the sick to health, release the tormented from devils, and transform the depraved to devoted disciples. They had seen His mind-boggling power, yet when they were confronted with this enemy that they had come to respect and fear, they doubted the Lord's strength against such a formidable foe. The fact that Jesus had allowed these disciples, many of them fishermen by trade, to face one of their greatest fears did not suggest that He was uncaring or detached. Rather, it demonstrated to them that they could face anything—as long as He was with them. His compassionate response to their cries actually validated His love and care.

3. Jesus *said* they would go to the other side. He gave His Word. Had they possessed any spiritual discernment, they would have believed what He said about Himself to be true: "*I and my Father are one.*" Jesus is God, and God cannot lie. His Word can be trusted.

You can trust Him too, "*For all the promises of God in him are yea, and in him Amen, unto the glory of God by us*" (2 Corinthians 1:20). In the Bible you can find thousands of promises about which you can say with confidence, "This is mine." Hebrews 13:5 is one such promise, a wonderful, wonderful verse that you ought to underline in your Bible. It says, "*Let your conversation* [meaning your manner of life or conduct] *be without covetousness; and be content with such things as ye have: for he hath said, I will never leave thee nor forsake thee.*" He has promised to be with you. Christian, doesn't that give you comfort? It ought to! No matter where you go or what you face, Jesus has promised that He will never leave you nor forsake you, and He is well able to calm any storm that assails.

Even though the disciples' circumstances looked bleak, each one could rest in these three facts, the same three that you and I must keep in mind during hardships: Jesus is with me; He is bigger than any problem I face, and I can trust His Word.

Why Do You Feel the Way You Do?

As I said before, feelings are nothing more than feelings, but if you do feel isolated and alone, there is a reason. You are the only one who can determine why you feel as you do. I encourage you to examine your own heart in the light of God's Word and then apply the remedy that meets your need.

Ask yourself these questions:

1. Am I living apart from God? In Hebrews 4:13 the Bible says, "*...the eyes of him with whom we have to do*" are always open. Our actions, thoughts, and motives are seen by God who judges us. The Old Testament prophet Isaiah said, "*But your iniquities have separated between you and your God, and your sins have hid his face from you, that he will not hear*" (Isaiah 59:2). Your sin has separated you from God, and without a Mediator you will be separated from Him for all eternity in a place called Hell.

Maybe you believe that a merciful God wouldn't send anyone to Hell. Maybe you are trusting in your good works to get you to Heaven. Maybe you are trusting your religion to save you. In any case, your trust is misplaced. The Bible teaches us that we are to place our trust in Christ, and Him alone, for our salvation. Each of us has a responsibility to obey this teaching, and everyone who does not accept Jesus as his Saviour will have to give an account to God for why he rejected Christ.

If you are an unbeliever who feels isolated and helpless, it is because you *are* isolated and helpless. That's why you feel lost and don't know where to turn. But at least you're not hopeless. God is ready to save you. He is a prayer away with peace that passes understanding, peace that can be yours for the asking.

"*...Believe on the Lord Jesus Christ, and thou shalt be saved*" (Acts 16:31). It is by faith in Jesus that you obtain salvation. You must realize that you can do nothing to save yourself from the penalty of your sin and believe that Jesus, God's Son, died in your place to pay the penalty you deserve. Then simply call on Him to save you: "Lord, here's my life. I give myself to

You. I ask You to forgive me of my sins and save my soul." God is standing there with outstretched arms, waiting for you to come to Him. He will save you, if you will just trust His Son.

The storms of life will do one of two things. The storms will lead you to dependence upon self as you live in isolation from God, or the storms of life will lead you to understand that you need to live your life in dependence upon God. Total dependence upon Him is what He wants from your life and mine.

When we feel all alone, that's the time to look to the Lord, to the one who cares about us, the one who will never leave us nor forsake us.

2. Have I allowed my affections to stray? Even a believer can feel far away from God if he has allowed his affections to stray.

The Bible warns us of our propensity to forsake God because of love for this world. "*For Demas hath forsaken me; having loved this present world*" (2 Timothy 4:10). Christian, our concern ought to be to guard our hearts diligently because our hearts are prone to wander away from God. We live in this world where the devil has many allurements to captivate our affection. If we are not careful, we will fall in love with all that this world has to offer—money, entertainment, glamour, and lust—and forget the God who loved us so much that He sent His Son to die for us. When our hearts are far from Him, it is easy to believe that we have been forsaken, especially when the storm comes and it seems as though we are facing it alone.

3. Do I lack faith? Have enough faith to trust Him even when your feelings tell you otherwise. In Mark 4:40, Jesus gently rebuked His disciples: "*Why are ye so fearful? how is it that ye have no faith?*" The emotions they were experiencing in the midst of the storm had caused them to stray from the truth: Jesus is with us; everything will be okay. Instead of trusting, they felt forsaken and alone.

During the storm your emotions tell you, "I've been abandoned; God has distanced Himself from me." You may feel like God has left you alone because the real truth has been shrouded by your pain or fear or grief. During such times, fill your heart with the truth of God's Word so that you can overcome your feelings with faith.

Mark it down. According to the Scriptures, God has not forsaken you. *"For the LORD loveth judgment, and forsaketh not his saints; they are preserved forever: but the seed of the wicked shall be cut off"* (Psalm 37:28). You can believe He cares. First Peter 5:7 says, *"Casting all your care upon him; for He careth for you."* Think about that—He cares for you. The God who created Heaven and earth cares for *you*! If He cares about everything that happens to the little sparrow, He certainly cares about every detail of your life.

Keep your heart fixed on the Truth lest you forget who He is—a God who loves and cares for you, a God who works everything for your good—even life's storms.

Conclusion

At best, the storms of life are inconvenient; at worst, they are downright terrifying. For those reasons, we hate storms. When they come, we get angry and rebel, or we try with childish simplicity to wish them away, but these things are to no avail. Trials are an inevitable part of our lives.

The truth is we *need* these storms. They are for our good, and God is right there with us to offer His help through the trial. But our human temptation is to take matters into our own hands and struggle in our own strength. Then when our self-effort fails, we feel that God has forsaken us or, worse, that He is actually trying to hurt us.

If we learn to put our trials in the proper perspective, if we understand that He is with us and that He is strong and capable, we will not feel forsaken and alone; rather we will feel loved and cared for, even in the storm.

2

When You Feel Out of Love with Your Spouse

MALACHI 2:11–17

Judah hath dealt treacherously, and an abomination is committed in Israel and in Jerusalem; for Judah hath profaned the holiness of the LORD which he loved, and hath married the daughter of a strange god. The LORD will cut off the man that doeth this, the master and the scholar, out of the tabernacles of Jacob, and him that offereth an offering unto the LORD of hosts. And this have ye done again, covering the altar of the LORD with tears, with weeping, and with crying out, insomuch that he regardeth not the offering any more, or receiveth it with good will at your hand. Yet ye say, Wherefore? Because the LORD hath been witness between thee and the wife of thy youth, against whom thou hast dealt treacherously: yet is she thy companion, and the wife of thy covenant. And did not he make one? Yet had he the residue of the spirit. And wherefore one? That he might seek a godly seed. Therefore take heed to your spirit, and let none deal treacherously against the wife of his youth. For the LORD, the God of Israel, saith that he hateth putting away: for one covereth violence with his garment, saith the LORD of hosts: therefore take heed to your spirit, that ye deal not treacherously. Ye have wearied the LORD with your words. Yet ye say, Wherein have we wearied him? When ye say, Every one that doeth evil is good in the sight of the LORD, and he delighteth in them; or, Where is the God of judgment?

American homes are in crisis today as divorce rates skyrocket. It seems as though many consider divorce an inalienable right—one of the freedoms guaranteed to us by the Constitution of the United States. Unfortunately, we find the same mindset among professed "born again" Christians whose divorce rate corresponds closely with the soaring national average. What is happening to the American psyche that allows the destruction of the home without remorse for devastating a spouse, injuring innocent children, and grieving the Saviour who died for us?

Marriage Is Work

In my thirty-five years of pastoring and counseling experience, I believe I have dealt with about every kind of problem a couple can have. Frankly, in my more than forty-six years of marriage, I have had many problems to work through with my own marriage. Does that surprise you? I can almost hear your deprecation. "You mean to tell me that preachers have marital problems?" Yes, we do.

In every marriage, problems arise between the husband and wife. For some, those problems arise almost daily. The truth is, however, that problems never destroy a marriage. Trying to live with unresolved problems is what destroys a marriage. This is true in your marriage, and it is true in mine. If my wife and I were to allow problems to go unresolved, our marriage would be on the rocks too. But I tell you this honestly: not a single problem exists between my wife and me today because we have made a habit of dealing with each one as it arises. By following the principles set down in the Word of God, my wife and I, with God's help, enjoy a problem-free marriage.

It is absolutely true, that if you and your spouse will follow the same principles, you too will have a marriage free of turmoil and strife. "But," you say, "that's just not the real world because everyone has marital problems, and plenty of them." Sadly, that may be the way it is, but that's not the way it has to be. If you and your spouse make a commitment never to let a problem remain unresolved, you can have a marriage that is more heavenly than stormy—a marriage full of rainbows.

In response to the guy that said, "Marriages are made in Heaven," the cynic retorted, "Oh yeah? Well, so are thunder and lightning!" Remember this: when the sun breaks through the clouds after all the thunder and lightning, a beautiful rainbow often appears as a reminder of God's faithfulness to His promises.

God has not breached His promises concerning the blessings of marriage. His plan is not flawed. Then why are so many marriages failing? One counselor said, "There are basically only two things that cause unhappy marriages—men and women!" I suppose he meant that the obstacle standing in the way of a wonderful marriage relationship is the two people involved. But the truth is you can change—with God's help. You can be in love with your spouse, even if the feelings you are experiencing now tell you otherwise. I want to show you how. If you will read the entire chapter and then work at practicing the principles therein, you will see—and feel—a difference in your marriage. I promise.

Your attitude at the outset of this reading will determine the end result. Let's look at one couple's marriage relationship to illustrate the importance of attitude. Michael and Sarah have been struggling through some contention that has strained the marriage. Sarah is ready to throw in the towel, but Michael, realizing his own shortcomings, has determined to be the blessing to his wife that he should have been all along. He sets out to do little things to show her that he loves her: flowers, notes, sweet words, acts of kindness, but nothing he can say or do changes her heart.

Why is that? The reason Sarah is untouched is the attitude she clings to. With a bitter heart, she says, "I dare you to be a blessing to me!" It is Sarah's wrong attitude that is at fault, not Michael's failure to offer affection.

The same thing could be true of you as you read this chapter. If your attitude is "I don't care what this chapter says, my marriage is too far gone to be helped," you're probably right. If you have the attitude, "There is no point in trying. There's no love left to salvage," there probably never will be. If you come to this chapter saying, "I dare you to teach me something that will change my feelings for my spouse," you probably will never change. If, however, you read this chapter with the attitude, "I'd like to learn something, and I am willing to change," then God can do something that you never thought possible.

It will be a battle, but God is well able to win the victory. You must, therefore, prepare yourself for warfare by learning Satan's tactics for destroying marriages. He has an arsenal of weapons to hurl at marriages, yet he has nothing new.

As we study the stiff-necked Israelites in the book of Malachi and the many ways they offended God, we find what looks more like an editorial commentary on America today than something that took place 2,400 years ago. Satan is using the same strategies he has been using for thousands of years. Rather than repeat history, let's learn from the problems these people experienced and determine to leave no unresolved problems in our own marriages.

There Are No New Problems

The Old Testament prophet Malachi, whose name literally means "messenger," came to Judah (the Jews of Israel) with a message from God: "*Judah hath dealt treacherously, and an abomination is committed in Israel and in Jerusalem; for Judah hath profaned the holiness of the* Lord *which he loved, and hath married the daughter of a strange god*" (Malachi 2:11).

It seems that the inhabitants of Judah, having already spent years in captivity because of their wickedness, still had not learned their lessons.

They had defiled themselves by worshipping false deities, and though God had warned His people over and over about their sin, and though He waited patiently for them to return to Him, they would not. Because of their unwillingness to repent, God allowed their conquest, and the people were taken into captivity by the Babylonians around 600 BC.

During their Babylonian captivity, God orchestrated the fall of Babylon to Cyrus, king of Persia, and at His appointed time, God moved the heart of Cyrus to decree that the Jews be permitted to return to Jerusalem in Judah, at which time some of the people did return.

But during their seventy years of captivity, the land had not been left empty. Other people—heathens who worshipped false gods and practiced pagan religions—moved into the land, and now the Jews who had returned to the area from Babylon, influenced by these idolatrous people, were committing an abomination, something absolutely detestable and abhorrent to Almighty God, so much so that God sent Malachi to them with His message: *"Judah hath dealt treacherously, and an abomination is committed in Israel and in Jerusalem."* What was it that God found to be so offensive?

PROBLEM #1: DISREGARD FOR GOD'S HOLINESS

A man's concept of God's holiness determines his attitude toward sin. When a man forgets that God is holy and that He abhors and judges sin, he is easily drawn into every kind of deplorable musing and action with no thought for how his sin heaps profound grief upon God or inevitable consequences upon himself.

In Malachi 2, we find Judah in this condition. These people, chosen by God to be His very own, had lost their reverence and respect for Him. Their blatant disregard had manifested itself into actions God called treacherous and abominable, actions that profaned His very holiness. They intermarried with pagans, *"the daughter of a strange god."*

God was very adamant that the nation of Israel not be corrupted by the surrounding nations and their heathen idolatry because Israel was the nation and people through which He would send the Messiah to the world. God had specifically told the Jews that they were never to marry outside the Jewish nation, yet they blatantly violated God's specific restriction because they didn't care about God, His holiness, or His Word.

American culture has deteriorated to the point that we have assumed, even embraced, the same irreverent attitude toward God. We go so far as to boldly emblazon our clothing with this attitude—"No Fear." It is all too true that we have lost our fear of God, and sadly, we see this lack of fear manifested in the obvious disregard that even professing Christians have for God's Word, the appalling divorce rate amongst Christians being only one example. But, really, our sin runs deeper than that. If we choose to look where God looks—our hearts—we will find what is at the root of it all: pride, bitterness, selfishness, and envy, to name just a few.

Though we do not see our sin as deplorable, God does. In verse 12, we see how God feels about the sins of His people, sins that hinder our human relationships and, worse, our relationship with God: "*The Lord will cut off the man that doeth this, the master and the scholar.*" The persons mentioned here are those who profaned the holiness of God in marrying ungodly heathens who did not believe in the God of Israel. God said, "I'll cut off the man that does this, anyone and everyone." He further added that He would not receive their offering brought with tears.

We cannot expect that God will receive our offering of prayers if we choose to disrespect and profane the holiness of God in clinging to our pride and all the sin that it engenders. Obedience to God and His Word is imperative to having a blessed and happy marriage.

PROBLEM #2: AN UNREPENTANT SPIRIT

I want to make a quick point of clarification before we discuss repentance. In Malachi 2, we are looking at God's chosen people, those who have a relationship with God. God deals with His people quite differently from how He deals with unbelievers. It doesn't surprise God when sinners sin—it shouldn't surprise us either—and He does not shut His ears to a prayer of repentance. He will always hear the prayer of an unsaved person calling on His name for salvation from sin.

When a believer, however, acts in a manner disrespectful toward God, when he commits any sin, the fellowship between that believer and God is broken. God tells His people in this passage that until they repent of their sin, He will not listen to their cries, nor will He accept their offerings of worship. *"And this have ye done again, covering the altar of the LORD with tears, with weeping, and with crying out, insomuch that he regardeth not the offering any more, or receiveth it with good will at your hand"* (Malachi 2:13). He is unimpressed by their show of tears. Repentance is what He requires of His erring people, and repentance, as we will discuss later, will be a huge step toward a loving relationship with your spouse.

PROBLEM #3: BROKEN VOWS

The Bible said that the men were not only marrying unbelieving women but also divorcing their own wives to do it. It seems that upon returning to Judah, many of these men became enamored with the heathen women that occupied the land, and their wives suddenly did not look so desirable. "I don't want this old wife I brought back from Babylon," they thought. "I want a new model." I suppose their reasons for acting in this abominable way are the same reasons people have today. The new prospect is more appealing—maybe younger or sexier. Whatever the process of thinking, this sin became widespread as people adopted the "everyone is doing it" mindset.

The people profaned the holiness of the Lord not only in disregarding His commandment concerning intermarriage but also in breaching the vows they had sworn before their God. These vows were a holy obligation.

Marriage is a covenant, a promise. Therefore, when a man and woman stand before God to vow, "I promise, till death do us part, to be your loving and faithful husband (or wife)," they are making a covenant before God. God witnesses the oath and joins them together as one flesh—for life. It is then that they are recognized as husband and wife. In God's eyes, they are as married at that moment as they will be after their honeymoon because marriage is not based on sex, but on the covenant. God said that in breaking this vow, the Israelites were dealing treacherously with their wives and committing an act that He hates.

God reminds them in the last half of the verse 14, *"yet is she thy companion, and the wife of thy covenant."* Once a man and a woman enter into a marriage covenant—a promise before God to be joined to the other person—that is the end of the matter. You ought to underline that in your Bible, circle it, and put a star by it. If you don't get anything else from this chapter, please get this one point from the Word of God: your marriage is a covenant, a solemn promise entered into together, a promise to stay married to one another until death. That is God's plan for marriage—together forever. Marriage is about being true to your promise. Feelings of love may come or go, but the promise is forever.

God has not changed His mind on this matter. In His eyes, the original marriage is the only legitimate marriage. When we stand before Him to vow "until death us do part," God still views this vow as sacred, and He still views divorce as a sin against the spouse and against Him.

PROBLEM #4: PRETENTIOUS WORSHIP

The people decided they were going to do the things they wanted to do and live the way they wanted to live. Even so, they continued going to the temple as though nothing had changed. God said, "You who are profaning my holiness by divorcing your wives and intermarrying with the heathen, I cannot bless you."

They responded with a question—as if God had not already spoken very plainly through His prophet—*"Wherefore?"* In one word they were asking, "But wait a minute, God. What wrong have we done? Look what we are doing to please you. We're coming here to the place of worship and offering up our offerings. What's more, we are coming with a flood of tears."

Do you see the hypocrisy in what they were saying and doing? These men, after they had dumped their wives and married heathen women, went to the temple to offer their sacrifices at the altar and cry out to the very God whom they were disrespecting with their sin.

God said, "You have wearied Me. With blatant disregard for morality and righteousness, you have disobeyed Me, the one you claim to be your God; therefore, My ears are stopped to your cries."

PROBLEM #5: ERRONEOUS NOTIONS

For most couples, the first thing that drew them to their spouse was a physical chemistry—that tingle that zipped down their spine at the thought of their sweetheart, the light-headed fuzziness and heart palpitations that caused them to swoon. Before long, their attraction grew into obsession. They couldn't bear to be apart. He couldn't get enough of her alluring eyes. She couldn't get enough of his disarming smile. If you asked either of the people if they thought their spouse was attractive way back when, the answer would be an enthusiastic, "Yes!"

But all too often I hear couples complain, "The feeling is gone." I am not denying that these feelings are powerful and exciting. The early days of romance are full of bliss. But our society promotes the idea that those strong feelings and physical attraction are what make the relationship meaningful. Americans have become so addicted to pleasure that they need another "fix" when that initial ecstasy begins to wane. After all, who wants to be stuck in a boring, ho-hum relationship?

Another remark that I have heard from discontented spouses is, "She (or he) is no longer attractive to me." The remedy for that complaint is simply to go stand in front of a mirror and look at yourself objectively. Try to see what your spouse is stuck with before you start condemning!

Are you the man or woman that your spouse married five, ten, thirty years ago?

Wrinkles and pounds do creep in. Problems and responsibilities may douse the fire. You may not be what you used to be, but physical "chemistry" ought to have nothing to do with the condition of your marriage. The Bible doesn't say that we stay married only until we wrinkle and sag. No! It says until death do us part (1 Corinthians 7:39).

Actually, we have it good. In some countries, particularly in the Middle East, marriages are arranged. Because the parents are the ones making the arrangements, the bride and groom sometimes do not meet until they are standing at the wedding altar. I can only imagine what that would be like.

When I was a kid, they sold Cracker Jacks in waxed boxes for a nickel. Inside every box there was a little gift wrapped in paper. I unwrapped my little trinket, and if I didn't like it, I swapped it for some other guy's prize. That must be what it's like for some of those guys that have never seen their wives before the wedding. Can you imagine the groom sighing, "Man, I hope I've got a good prize under this veil"?

Most of us in America are not involved in arranged marriages. We had ample opportunity to scrutinize our spouses before marriage. Allow me to remind you, you chose your spouse, and you vowed to God to stay true until death.

PROBLEM #6: UNGIVING SPIRIT

I've also heard people say, "Well, I just don't feel like I love my spouse anymore." I'll address their grievance with a question: "What do feelings have to do with marriage?" I'm serious! Certainly you would like to feel love as a part of your marital relationship, but feelings are never the reason for staying married. A marriage cannot be based on something as changeable as emotion.

In some marriage relationships, problems have been so severe or have remained unresolved for so long that, where there was affection, there is now loathing, where there was tenderness, there is now spite. Feelings can swing from one end of the pendulum to the other. Such was the case of King David and his first wife, Michal. They had everything going for them. King David was enjoying great victory. Michal was married to a handsome, powerful king. They had everything money could buy. But their feelings for one another had diminished to the point that Michal absolutely despised David (2 Samuel 6:16; 1 Chronicles 15:29). What happened? What takes place in people's lives that they lose the love they once had for one another?

Many factors may contribute to this loss of love: incompatibilities, adversities, even infidelity; but what happens more often is that people simply quit investing in the relationship the way they did at the beginning. He's too insensitive to realize that she still needs to hear sweet nothings whispered in her ear. She's too busy with kids and housework to sit down and watch a ball game with him.

Couples often say, "There's nothing there. We've grown apart. We just don't have anything in common." Keep in mind, it takes two to be married, and if you and your spouse have grown apart, you are at least partially at fault. You say, "It's not my fault! It's my husband's fault," or "My wife is in the wrong." Neither of these statements is true. *You* have responsibilities to your marriage. If there's "nothing there," you're saying, "I am putting nothing into my marriage." Statements like that are an admission that you are not contributing to the relationship. When you persist in loving actions, loving feelings will follow. Feelings follow actions. It is a biblical principle that you love what you invest in. Matthew 6:21 says, *"For where your treasure is, there will your heart be also."*

I've got a simple little philosophy that you might find helpful: I'll get no more out of life than what I put into it. The same goes for marriage. What you put into it is what you'll get out of it.

PROBLEM #7: SELFISHNESS

In 1994, I read of a man named Firstenberg. From what I know, he was not a Christian man, and he wasn't necessarily speaking to Christian people when he made some studied observations about American culture. Nonetheless, I found some of his assertions to be noteworthy. He suggested that the 140-year pattern of continual growth in America's divorce rate—the highest in the world—is related to the "high cultural value" that Americans place on independence. He asserts that a culture that values independence encourages people to seek their own personal development rather than commitment to the family. It would be hard to argue that ours is not a culture that values independence over commitment to honoring one's covenants, especially the marital covenant. I have heard this statement myself from spouses who want out of their commitment: "Well, I feel trapped, and I want my independence."

I believe what the statistics really reflect is not so much a high value on independence as the magnitude to which selfishness has swelled in America as a dominating cultural malady. The stench of selfishness pervades a society when its people put their own interests above those of Almighty God. This is just my personal opinion, but I think we have the National Organization for Women to thank for the pervasiveness of this attitude in our lifetime.

Whatever the reason, it is clear that selfishness is the nemesis to healthy marriages. People often get married for selfish reasons in the first place. They imagine all that their partner will do to add to their own personal happiness, when in reality, they are committing to the other person's happiness when they take their vows. Marriage means that each partner in the relationship no longer has the freedom or luxury to think of himself first. Rather, each assumes responsibilities to the other as the couple commits to love and honor the other through sickness and health, poverty and wealth.

Some people just don't seem to understand this. I've seen many times in men, but in women as well, the attitude that says, "Why do I always have to go directly home? Why don't I have the freedom I used to have? I just can't take the pressures anymore." To these people I say, "You should have thought about what you were committing to before you got married." But you are married. That means it is time to learn how to emulate the mind of Christ, preferring others above yourself. Serving others is the only way to find the happiness our selfish hearts desire anyway.

PROBLEM #8: MARITAL DISCONTENTMENT

John shuffles into the office unhappy about himself because of the way he had left things at home. Instead of resolving—right away, before going to bed, as the Bible teaches—the issue he and his wife, Meg, had argued over the night before, he left her upset, standing there in her bathrobe, struggling to get crabby kids ready for school on her own. Even the poor children seemed to be reacting to the tension that filled the air.

He sets down his briefcase with a heavy sigh and plops down into his chair just as Julie from the next office appears in the doorway.

"Bad morning, huh?"

"Well, you know...."

Julie sits in the chair opposite John's desk and says, "I'm all ears."

As John relays the problems of that morning and the night before, he becomes aware of the soft scent of Julie's perfume. He can't help but notice how attractive she looks in the jade blouse she is wearing. "I never realized how green her eyes are," John thinks. She is quite a contrast to the disheveled wife he had left that morning.

Julie nods with a sympathetic smile. "I understand, John."

As she relates some of the same problems in her own marriage, John feels a little boost. It feels so good to know that someone else understands.

I'm sure you can imagine what ensued over the next few months as their meetings drew them closer together.

Unfortunately, this scenario is not uncommon. John and Julie are pretty typical. The initial excitement has faded in their marriages. At the same time, they are faced with pressures and responsibilities that take a toll on their relationships. They have two choices: stay and work on their existing marriages or take the "easy" way out and jump ship.

Is it any wonder that people jump ship, especially when the "lifesaver" looks so appealing? Think about our previous discussions regarding the ways our culture has influenced us: our addiction to pleasure, the prevalent me-first attitude, our irreverence toward God and His Word. Along with those, I could add our discontentment and our desire for instant gratification. These all add up to a people who lack the character to make the investment necessary to have a good marriage.

I've heard people say all too often, "I have found someone else." Whoever this someone else is, they are usually more understanding, more attractive, more fun, more exciting to be with than the current spouse. I'll say this as plainly as I can: if this is your way of thinking, it is a sinful and destructive thought pattern. This kind of thinking was prevalent among the Israelites in Micah 2, but God said: "*Judah hath dealt treacherously, and an abomination is committed in Israel and in Jerusalem*" (Malachi 2:11).

Unfortunately, this wickedness is permeating our society as well. But it doesn't matter what the rest of the world does; a Christian should counter the wicked influences of society with genuine Christianity—a real and vibrant walk with God. And he should safeguard himself against illicit relationships.

First, married people should not tell their innermost feelings about their spouse to anyone, particularly someone of the opposite gender. Reader, make it your rule to say only flattering remarks about your spouse. Griping and complaining to others is not the way to handle problems. If you need to talk to someone, go together to your pastor for counseling, and do what he tells you to do from the Word of God.

Next, safeguard yourself by avoiding situations where you are alone with someone of the opposite sex. Don't ever go out to lunch or to dinner with somebody of the opposite sex—for any reason—unless you have a crowd at your table. It's fine to participate in office celebrations or meetings, but going alone with a person of the opposite sex is never proper. Do not make an opportunity for your affections to be turned away from your spouse and toward someone else.

You might say, "Wait a minute, that's just not the real world today. Everybody does it." Not true. There are many of us that keep much separation from the opposite sex. It doesn't take much for the devil to confuse us when we are in a vulnerable position, even when we think, "I'll never do that."

We cannot afford to get cocky or arrogant about our ability to withstand temptations. I doubt that anyone stands at the marriage altar thinking, "I wonder how long this will last before I have an affair with someone else?" Most people don't think their marriage will end up as one of the statistics. The norm is that people enter into a marriage thinking that it will last forever. That's why they get married! Temptation to cheat always comes up later.

Finally, I implore you to guard your heart, *"for out of it are the issues of life"* (Proverbs 4:23b). Every affair happens after a process of wicked thinking. It may seem innocent at first, one spouse dwelling on the other's faults, but those first thoughts of discontentment are the seeds that bring forth a bumper crop of heartache later. Keep your thoughts in subjection to the Lord, and allow Him to renew your mind through His Word.

Six Steps to Regaining Lost Ground

Perhaps you're thinking, "The fact is that I just do not love my spouse any longer." I have six suggestions that, if followed carefully, will rekindle the feeling of affection you once had for your spouse.

1. Make sure of your personal relationship with God. God made each of us with a spiritual vacuum, a God-shaped hole that only He can fill. The problem is that we try everything else to fill the void. People try to fill it with things. They go out and buy, buy, buy, but things don't satisfy. Many try alcohol or drugs, but it is only a temporary escape.

Religion is just one more thing that people try to ease the emptiness they feel. But religion is not the same as a relationship with God. Trying to fill the void with religion is like trying to put a square peg into a round hole. It just won't fit. No one but God can satisfy the longing you feel.

We must have a personal relationship with Him, but there is a huge chasm that separates us from God—our sin. The only way we can find our way to God is for Someone to bridge that gap. That's what Jesus did when He stretched out His arms on an old rugged cross to die for our sins. He reached one hand to God and the other to us as He took the punishment for our sins so that we could be forgiven and reconciled to God. If you have never placed your faith in Jesus as your Saviour, you will continue to search in vain for satisfaction until you do. And sadly, you will miss the grace He wants to give you to help in all your other relationships. No other relationship can ever be exactly what God intends it to be if you do not have a relationship with Him.

2. Consider God's perspective on divorce. If you had a conversation with God about His opinion on divorce, it might go something like this:

"God, what do You think about divorce?"

"I hate it."

You continue, "Well, of course You do, but what about special cases? For example, what about the husband and wife who have tried to make it work for years but just can't seem to find common ground? They are always bickering and battling, even with children in the home. They are both fed up! What do you think about divorce then?"

"I hate it," God repeats.

"Lord, what do You think when the husband turns out to be a slouch, a couch potato, a complete jerk. Having put up with mistreatment all these years for the sake of the children, that man's wife would surely be justified in leaving once the kids are grown up and gone, right?"

God says, "I hate divorce."

"But God, when a wife has lost her sex appeal and doesn't try to understand her husband's needs, don't You think divorce is the best option in that case?

"I hate it," God says once again.

Look at Malachi 2:16. The prophet says, *"For the LORD, the God of Israel, saith that he hateth putting away."* Think about it carefully. You had better be very careful about calling something good that God calls evil. Unless there is the biblical ground of adultery, according to Matthew 19:9 and Matthew 5:32, then divorce simply is not an option, especially for someone who loves God.

3. Make a list of ways you have failed in your marriage. You say, "You don't get it, preacher! The problem is not me; it's my spouse."

To this I respond, "Let me talk to your spouse to see what he/she has to say about the problems in your marriage." Two people always have two different ways of looking at things.

Since you can do nothing to change your spouse, your own failures are a good place to begin. Analyzing your own actions and attitudes can be very telling. When you make your list, you may not see your failures as being the direct cause of your problems, but putting them on paper may be more revealing than you would have guessed. It may be that the problem is related to your spouse's reaction to your failure. Sometimes problems become more obvious when you simply take the time to analyze them.

What would happen if you agreed to examine your marriage to see where the problems may have started or how they were made worse by your own action or response? What would happen if your spouse made the same evaluation? If, at the very first sign of a problem in the marriage, you simply said, "Let me figure out how I have, perhaps, failed my marriage," and set out to work on those things, you might find out your home would be a better place to live, even for you.

4. Confess your failures to God and to your spouse. When any relationship has been breached, the only way to reconcile the people involved is with honesty. Full disclosure is imperative to clear the air. You must tell your spouse honestly what you have done and ask for forgiveness. You must also be honest with your spouse about the pain he/

she may have caused you, and then offer forgiveness. Once it is out, let it go. Forgiveness is the key to this whole scenario.

Resolve to let God change you and your marriage. Notice I said to let God make the change. You can't change yourself, and it is certainly true that you can't change your spouse! You need the power of the Holy Spirit to help you to forgive graciously, to love generously, and to break old habits and thought patterns that have controlled you for years. This filling requires that both you and your spouse know Jesus Christ as your personal Saviour and that you fill yourselves with His Word. You will be amazed at the change He will make in you when you allow Him to do His work.

Marriage is teamwork. It takes two people, a husband and a wife along with God Almighty, doing the work in your lives and your marriage. It requires a willingness to communicate honestly and openly because you will both be dealing with tough issues. Finally, it may take the help of a godly counselor. Do not hesitate to ask your pastor to help you work on your marriage or to suggest a Christian counselor for you. I might add this: a counselor will not help if you do not follow his advice. Take the steps necessary to mend your marriage.

5. Set your focus in the right place. Anytime a person contemplates leaving a marriage, it is certain that the person is thinking selfishly without regard for how divorce will impact the spouse or the children: "I can't stay with her," "I don't love him," or "I want to be with this other person." Notice all the I's? This selfish way of thinking is—plain and simple—pride. And God hates it. There is nothing He hates more.

Crushing your pride is very difficult to do because it involves changing stubborn thought patterns and attitudes. So, what is the remedy? I heard someone say, "Pride is not thinking less of yourself; it's not thinking of yourself at all." When your thoughts turn to what you want, what you're missing, how you've been mistreated, or how you deserve more, stop and ask God to forgive you for your pride and then redirect your thinking. Take your focus off yourself and put it on God first, then on your spouse, and finally, on any children that God may have given to you. Turning the focus away from self makes selfish thoughts impossible.

"But," you say, "I just can't. The feelings of love just are not there anymore." Feelings have nothing to do with it. You can change your attitude, with God's help. *"I can do all things through Christ which strengtheneth me"* (Philippians 4:13). You can do anything God wants you to do, and it is certain that God wants you to mend your marriage. You do your part, filling yourself with His Word and begging Him for help, and God will do His, changing your heart. That's His department. Let Him do His job. Trust that He will.

6. Remember that marriage is a companionship. Refer again to Malachi 2:14: *"yet is she thy companion, and the wife of thy covenant."* Plan time and activities for companionship. I suggest making a list of things you can do together. Plan some dates, invite people to your home, go shopping, play games—find something! But keep in mind, not everybody agrees. I found out the first time I ever played football with my wife that she didn't like it. It wasn't her thing. Now we both love playing golf. Well, she doesn't quite see it the way I do yet, but we're working on it.

There are some activities you may want to avoid completely. My wife loved wallpaper in the house. I tried to hang wallpaper with her in one of the bathrooms. That's the closest to divorce we've ever come! I'll never do it again, ever! That activity was not a good companionship builder. But do figure out what it is you enjoy doing, and do it together.

You don't have to spend a lot of money. Maybe you could start taking walks, riding bicycles, or any number of things that cost nothing—nothing, that is, but time. Time is the one investment you must make. You'll never develop companionship without investing time. If you don't have time for your spouse, make time.

Here's your homework: take a moment, put down this book and write down twenty things you and your spouse can do together. Ask your spouse to make a list and then share the lists with each other. See if you can find something you agree on—something, anything, and do it.

Remember, where you invest your time and treasure is where your heart will be. I suggest that you invest in the most important human relationship God gave you.

A Final Thought

So, how are you going to deal with how you feel when you feel out of love with your spouse? It's up to you. Here are the choices that you have to make: You can either resort to your old selfish and fleshly sin nature, or you can give yourself over to God and to your spouse. You can continue trying to fix your marriage on your own, or you can let God work through you. You can hold on to the hurt of old wounds, or you can choose to forgive the way Christ forgave you. You can merely endure your marriage, or you can give yourself wholeheartedly to your spouse and start having a fantastic marriage, right now.

It is a wonderful feeling to be madly in love with your spouse. I highly recommend it. You can have that kind of relationship if you are willing do your part and let God do His.

3

When You Feel Totally Depressed

Depression dominates the lives of many people—tens of millions, in fact. Some people are hit by an episode of depression, but are able to work through it. Others suffer prolonged bouts. If you have not had to deal with depression, it may be that your time to confront this monster is yet in the future, but at one time or another, we will all face the temptation to succumb to its control.

Depression is a complex issue that can have a host of contributing causes. I am not a doctor, and I do not claim to be an expert on the rare physiological contributors to depression. In these cases, I would recommend you seek the evaluation of a qualified medical doctor. In this chapter, I am solely focusing on the spiritual and emotional causes. God's Word does in fact have much to say about discouragement and depression.

PSALM 42:1–11

As the hart panteth after the water brooks, so panteth my soul after thee, O God. My soul thirsteth for God, for the living God: when shall I come and appear before God? My tears have been my meat day and night, while they continually say unto me, Where is thy God? When I remember these things, I pour out my soul in me: for I had gone with the multitude, I went with them to the house of God, with the voice of joy and praise, with a multitude that kept holyday. Why art thou cast down, O my soul? and why art thou disquieted in me? hope thou in God: for I shall yet praise him for the help of his countenance. O my God, my soul is cast down within me: therefore will I remember thee from the land of Jordan, and of the Hermonites, from the hill Mizar. Deep calleth unto deep at the noise of thy waterspouts: all thy waves and thy billows are gone over me. Yet the LORD will command his lovingkindness in the daytime, and in the night his song shall be with me, and my prayer unto the God of my life. I will say unto God my rock, Why hast thou forgotten me? why go I mourning because of the oppression of the enemy? As with a sword in my bones, mine enemies reproach me; while they say daily unto me, Where is thy God? Why art thou cast down, O my soul? and why art thou disquieted within me? hope thou in God: for I shall yet praise him, who is the health of my countenance, and my God.

No one escapes difficulties, not even a pastor. For over thirty-five years, I ministered in the same place. Having traveled that familiar road for so long, I saw many mountaintops, but I also traveled through many valleys as well. The work of a pastor has its ups and its downs—the building program that we attempted to start twice in ten years comes to mind here—and during the uphill climbs, I often grew weary. I did, and still do, experience sorrow, confusion, and discouragement just as everyone else. After all, I've got a heart! When life gets difficult, I am prone to think, "Hey, what's this all about?"

Discouraged, but Not Depressed

As everyone else, I can have times of discouragement. As a spiritual leader, however, I have sought to keep my heart in check so that I do not allow my personal discouragements to lead me to a point where I am unable to bear the burdens of others. If I allow myself to sink into a pit of spiritual depression, I am not only hurting myself but those I lead. God instructs us to choose to rejoice in Him.

We do not have to be a victim of our circumstances, nor do we have to be a slave to our feelings. If you are, you will be up today but down tomorrow. You'll have the Elijah complex (1 Kings 18:21–19:10): you'll be up on top of the mountain, aware of God's hand on your life, and then, almost instantly, you'll be down in the valley, asking God to take your life. That is not how God wants us to live.

How do you handle life when you didn't get your promotion, your spouse gained a hundred pounds, your dog bit you, and your kid ran away? Maybe you made up your mind to invest in the stock market just in time for the Dow Jones® to plummet. Nothing is working out! You're losing your job, someone hit your car at church where everyone is supposed to be sanctified, and to top it all off, when you open your Bible to find some encouragement, your scheduled reading plan dictates the first nine chapters of 1 Chronicles with all the genealogies. It's tempting to think, "Nothing in my life is working out. Why is all this happening to me?"

To be brutally frank, I get tired of people saying, "Life is really a bum deal." It's true that life can be tough. Everybody has problems. I have a different set of problems from yours, but we all have them. If you let all the circumstances weigh upon you, your shoulders will droop as if you are carrying the weight of the world. You'll become a defeated individual, but you don't have to be. Whatever happens, you do not have to become depressed.

Facing Problems without Depression

Psalm 42 provides some helpful counsel for someone going through depression. It is a passage that was most likely written while David was in exile either in Arum (Syria) or Babylon (Iraq). Although no one can say for sure exactly what problem David was facing, it seems as though he was taunted by captors, for his enemies repeatedly asked, "Where is thy God, David?" You're supposed to have this God who can do miraculous things. Where is He?"

Because he was away from a vital source of encouragement—the house of God and the people of God—David struggled to remind himself of where his hope was, "*Why art thou cast down, oh my soul? Why art thou disquieted within me? hope thou in God.*" David began to feel discouraged to the point that he asked God, "*Why hast thou forgotten me?*" It seems that, at this point, depression had set in.

Depression Defined

What is depression? To understand what depression is, it is important to understand what depression is not. Depression is not merely disappointment or discouragement or a slight case of the blues. Those things are common experiences to everyone. The disciples who fished for a living had bad days when they didn't catch much. Those meager catches that imperiled their very livelihood caused discouragement, but not depression. The Apostle Paul certainly understood difficulty. He said, "*We are troubled on every side, yet not distressed; we are perplexed, but not in despair; Persecuted, but not forsaken; cast down, but not destroyed*" (2 Corinthians 4:8–9). Paul said, "I am enduring some very difficult trials for my Lord. I am not, however, allowing these things to defeat me. I will keep going for God."

Of course, the example we always want to look to is our Lord. When Jesus was about to heal the man of his withered hand, the Pharisees were looking for an opportunity to accuse Him. The Bible says in Mark 3:5, "*And when he* [Jesus] *had looked round about on them with anger, being grieved for the hardness of their hearts.*" If you read this and other stories, you will see that Jesus was grieved by people's hard hearts, saddened at their lack of faith, and angered by their irreverence. He was scorned, accused, and conspired against, but with all the discouragements He faced here on Earth, He was never depressed, because depression was not an option.

Depression is not mental illness. In his book *The Christian Counselor's Manual* professional Christian counselor Jay Adams indicates that depression is often the result of a sinful response to life's problems:

> Depression is not inevitable, something that simply happens and cannot be avoided. Nor is it ever so far gone that the depression cannot be counteracted. The cycle can always be reversed at any point by biblical action in the power of the Holy Spirit. The hope for depressed persons, as elsewhere, lies in this: the depression is the result of the counselee's sin. If depression were some strange, unaccountable malady that has overcome him, for which he is not responsible and consequently about which he can do nothing, hope would evaporate. The fact is, however, though he may not be responsible for the initial problem (e.g., physical illness or a bad turn in his financial picture), he is responsible for *handling this initial problem God's way.* Because he hasn't, but instead has sinfully reacted to the problem (e.g., neglecting duties and chores; becoming resentful; complaining in self-pity), subsequently, *as a result of this reaction he has become depressed.*

Depression is a spirit of heaviness or gloom that lingers on and on, hovering like a dark cloud. People who give in to these feelings are consistently despondent because they believe they have lost control in a number of areas in their lives, not only in one. Eventually, those feelings of gloom do affect every area of life, making the depressed person dysfunctional at home, at the office, or in the community. He becomes convinced that he just doesn't relate to others and he has no worth because even the routine responsibilities of life are just too difficult to perform.

As this cycle of reactions and their repercussions snowball, depressed people even resort to suicide in an attempt to escape the oppression that they feel. In fact, studies have shown that the number one reason behind suicide is depression.

Suicide Is Not a Solution

Life can be tough, and people do have hard times. Shortly before I began this chapter, I saw an article in the newspapers about an incident at the Chesapeake Bay Bridge in Maryland. It is the world's longest continuous over-water steel bridge spanning 4.3 miles, and from the edge of the bridge, it's a long, long way down—about 200 feet. According to the paper, there was a traffic jam because people stopped to see what would happen when a desperate man stopped on the bridge, jumped out of his car, climbed over the railing, and balanced himself on the edge ready to jump a distance that would certainly take his life.

There was a uniformed policeman in the tie-up. He climbed over the railing himself and started inching closer to the guy so that he could talk to him. "I just want to help," he yelled when he was within just a few feet.

The guy said, "Hold it! Don't come any closer, or I'm going to jump!"

The police officer, obviously concerned for the man, said, "Sir, things can't be that bad."

The man said, "Oh, yes, they are."

"Tell me what's happening in your life," the policeman coaxed.

"Well," the man said, "my business just went bankrupt, and when my wife found out about it, she left me. Not only that, I don't have the money now to pay my mortgage." The guy went on and on unloading his burdens. Both of them clung to the edge of the bridge while onlookers held their breath. For thirty minutes the man and the officer talked.

The officer was finally able to talk the man down. The point is that this man had a mountain of problems—economic loss, bankruptcy, family problems—and the only way he could see to get out from under them was death. Problems, no matter how insurmountable they may seem, must be dealt with. Allowing your emotions to deteriorate to the point of depression only compounds matters. Take a look at your life. Are you taking positive steps to deal with the problems that are piling up, or are you crumbling beneath the weight? Do any of the following symptoms of depression describe you?

SYMPTOMS OF DEPRESSION

1. **Overwhelming sadness or tears.** Sometimes people cry and don't even know why. Self-absorption or self-pity is the number one problem. As they look inward, people become plagued with thoughts like these: "I can't believe he would do that to me," "I can't believe they fired me," or "I can't believe he hurt me that way." Please note that all the focus is on self.

2. **Inability to function.** "I've failed at this, and I've failed at that, so why go on?" What starts out as a sense of failure may snowball into a complete loss of interest, frustrating endeavors a person might otherwise attempt. A depressed person often loses interest in putting forth effort at anything whether it be on his job, at school, or at home, even when the effort involves his relationships.

3. **Disorderliness.** If a person who is generally neat allows everything to fall into disarray, he may be manifesting a warning sign of depression. His neat office or home is now sloppy. His usually tidy appearance is now disheveled. He may even become slack in his personal hygiene. His appearance says, "I just don't care anymore."

4. **Loss of appetite aside from a physical ailment.** The Bible records examples of such people. In 1 Samuel 1:8, we see Hannah so depressed over her barrenness that she refused to eat. Even her husband's expressions of deep love could not prevail over her profound sadness.

5. **Uncharacteristic abusive behavior—verbal or physical.** Both behaviors can take place when people become so exasperated with life's problems that they take their frustrations out on others by striking out.

This conduct is usually followed by excuse making or blame shifting. It's just never the fault of the abuser. It's always someone else's problem.

The Root of the Problem

What is at the spiritual root of this ongoing distress or despair? As I already mentioned, circumstances may start a person on the path toward depression. Usually those circumstances—of our own making or not—comprise what we might call "the hard knocks of life," but sometimes they are more than hard knocks; they are more like a crushing blow. Like an unexpected blow from a sledgehammer, tragic events sometimes devastate us without any warning at all. If the hard knocks start us on the path toward depression, the devastating blows push us downhill.

1. **Rejection.** This is often an overwhelming blow. God created us as social beings who need each other, and because love is such a basic need in our lives, rejection is an especially cruel difficulty to endure. Each of us has faced and will face rejection. Bullying from classmates, the betrayal of a dear friend, unrequited romantic love—all these cause severe pain, but a breach in our most intimate relationships causes *extreme* pain.

The parent/child relationship is one such relationship. Children who experience rejection by their parents—the very people who were supposed to love and protect them—often carry deep wounds into adulthood. The husband/wife relationship is another intimate relationship, perhaps the most intimate. When two people become one, the relationship cannot be severed without pain. Sometimes this pain develops into depression.

2. **Failing to achieve some goal.** Perhaps a student didn't make the athletic team or cheerleading squad, or wasn't accepted to the university from which parents and grandparents graduated. For some young people these goals are all that they have ever wanted from life or, more likely, all that their parents have ever wanted them to achieve. Having failed to achieve the goals that have always been expected of them, the children feel acute inadequacy and become depressed because

they are unable to handle what should have been nothing more than a painful discouragement.

3. Enduring severe criticism, especially continual criticism. Mark it down, you're going to be criticized, even if you serve God—and perhaps *particularly* if you serve God. You're going to have some problems and difficulties, but you have to make up your mind to stand on principle, though you will not please everyone.

As a pastor, I have been criticized nearly every day. Sometimes, pastors think they can please everyone and end up pleasing only a few. At the same time they are pleasing one group, they are displeasing another. That's life. I don't base my ministry on whether or not everyone, or anyone, likes my decisions. Although I pray my decisions will please people, my real goal is to please God, and whether your job entails full time Christian service or secular work, your goal should be the same.

4. Long-term illness. Struggling with frailty and severe pain over an extended period of time is grueling and sometimes causes people to want to end their lives prematurely. This circumstance is very depressing, especially for those who do not know what will become of them when this life ends.

5. Death of a loved one. This is perhaps the most devastating of these circumstances. My wife Mary and I were trying to reach out to neighbors where we previously lived. We visited one neighbor's home a couple of times and learned that the lady, almost a recluse, was just short of total depression, barely functioning well enough to receive us into her home. While we were talking to her, Mary realized the root of her depression. She had never recovered from the death of her mother nine years before. Having never received the help she needed, she sank lower and lower to the depressed state in which we found her, a state that literally defined who she was.

6. Personal sin and the individual's failure to deal with it. Consider Ahab in 1 Kings 21:4, *"And Ahab came into his house heavy and displeased because of the word which Naboth the Jezreelite had spoken to him: for he* *had said, I will not give thee the inheritance of my fathers. And he laid him down upon his bed, and turned away his face, and would eat no bread.*" Ahab had symptoms of what we might call classic depression—heaviness, isolation, and loss of appetite. Notice, however, that it was all brought on by sins such as discontent, greed, and anger toward God.

Consider Jonah as he prayed in Jonah 4:2, "*Therefore now, O LORD, take, I beseech thee, my life from me; for it is better for me to die than to live.*" Reading through this chapter, it is easy to spot self-pity at the root of Jonah's depression.

Recognizing sin as the root of depression can be difficult. We live in a society that points first to physical and emotional causes of depression. If you are depressed, it is more than likely you mishandled the circumstances God allowed to come into your life and ignored the comfort and hope God gives us through the burdens of life. You might say, "No, I feel the way I feel because I lost my mother." It is true that loss causes grief and pain, but prolonged, incapacitating sadness indicates an inward focus, a lack of faith, and an unbiblical perspective of life and of God Himself.

What about Medication?

The secular world often turns immediately to drugs, prescription or otherwise, as their solution for depression. The drug that is probably most often used is alcohol, since it brings immediate relief to a number of emotional and spiritual problems.

When there is a quantifiable physical problem, such as a chemical imbalance, as diagnosed by a physician, then it is wise to consider his advice. At the same time, one should immediately consult with his/her pastor. Often the physical problem is not the root problem, but a symptom of something spiritual (e.g., guilt, fear, anger, bitterness, hopelessness, slothfulness, rejection, etc.). The reason for seeking spiritual counsel (and I would do this first) along with medical counsel, is because some of the medical practitioners treat all of the above spiritual problems with drugs, which would slow down the recovery process greatly.

Obviously, if you have a broken arm, there is no sense in going to your pastor for help. You wouldn't want me, or any other pastor, to work on your broken bones! At the same time you need to be careful about going to a medical doctor when biblical counsel is what you need.

A Biblical Perspective Is the Key

It's important to remember that, as Jay Adams explained in his book *The Christian Counselor's Manual*, depression is not caused by the event but by the person's interpretation of and response to the event. Cultivating a biblical attitude is the key.

There is no person that can make me depressed. There is no circumstance that can make me depressed. "Well, suppose you wreck your car?" God knows what I need, and He will provide another, if I truly need it. "Suppose your house burns down?" God has it all worked out. "Well, suppose you miss opportunities. Suppose your building plans get turned down by the Board of Supervisors and you are not able to build for another ten years?" God has another plan. If we get turned down, we'll just have to try again and trust God for His timing which is exactly what we did.

I am thankful for the example of Christians who have maintained a good testimony through any circumstance. You might say, "Well, they just didn't have the adversities that I have had." That is not true. Think about the Apostle Paul. Through shipwrecks, hunger, beatings, and imprisonment, he didn't become depressed because he had developed godliness. He said, "I'll gladly take whatever God gives me because He has sacrificed so much for me. As long as I have Him, I have everything I need." If we are ever to overcome depression, we will have to develop godliness in our lives as well.

Deal with Depression Biblically

1. Establish a right relationship with the Lord. In Psalm 42:5 David questions, *"Why art thou cast down, O my soul? and why art thou disquieted within me?"* Then he says, *"hope thou in God."* Your hope for a right relationship must be in the right place or, in this case, in the right Person—Jesus Christ. Only trusting Christ as your personal Saviour can reconcile the broken relationship between you and God. When you come to know Him as your Saviour, you will realize that you can trust Him with your life as well, and then you truly will have hope in God to overcome your depression.

2. Acknowledge the Lord as the God of your life. Look at verse 8, *"Yet the Lord will command his lovingkindness in the daytime, and in the night his song shall be with me, and my prayer unto the God of my life."* David recognized that he must acknowledge the Lord as his God.

To overcome depression, you must do the same. Don't allow circumstances to dictate how you will live. Feelings are a good thing, but they do not determine how you run your life. There will be many times you may not feel like getting up, going to work, going to school, or asking forgiveness from someone you've wronged. You may not feel like doing the right thing, but you cannot allow your feelings to control you.

Anything that is allowed to control you, other than God, is a sin. When emotions fight for control in your life, you must deal with them as you would any other sin. Confess it to God and yield your emotions to His Holy Spirit.

Often the root problem is bitterness toward another person, which requires forgiveness. Sometimes it is anger toward God because life has not turned out the way you planned it. Whatever the problem, go to the Bible and follow God's directions for living. Allow Him to be God of *your* life.

3. Allow God to restructure your way of thinking. In Ephesians 4:23 the Bible talks about being *"renewed in the spirit of your mind."* The way you think about things and the way you approach life's circumstances are the keys to overcoming depression.

I read a story about two little league teams that were playing against each other. One of the teams was absolutely creaming the other team. It was really bad. A neighbor happened to walk by and saw one of the kids from his neighborhood playing.

He asked, "How is it going?"

"Well, it's not too bad," the player replied. "It's 18 to 0 in their favor."

The man said, "I can't believe you're not discouraged or depressed."

The little kid looked up and said, "Why should I be? We haven't been up to bat yet."

He had an optimistic way of thinking!

Maybe you've always had a pessimistic view of life, but with God's help, you *can* change the way you think.

Changing your thinking happens as you fill your mind with God's Word and focus your thoughts on Him and His loving kindness as the psalmist did in Psalm 42:6: *"O my God, my soul is cast down within me: therefore will I remember thee...."* When you find yourself returning to negative thoughts, confess your wrong thinking and refocus your thoughts on God. Singing spiritual songs is one good way to do this. David said in verse 8, *"in the night his song shall be with me."*

4. Focus your thoughts on others. The reason people get so down and eventually depressed is that they have their focus on the wrong person—themselves. They're always thinking about what's happening to them as opposed to what they can do to help others, and this inward focus causes feelings of gloom and despondency.

If you ever have a blue Monday, one quick antidote that will make a difference in how you feel is to *do* something for someone else. Honestly, serving others will make a difference in your outlook. You've probably heard the formula for joy: Jesus first, others second, yourself last=JOY. Your feelings largely center on where you choose to focus.

5. Change your attitude from one of negativity to one of praise. The latter part of verse 11 says, *"hope thou in God: for I shall yet praise him."* I can rejoice in every aspect of my life—in the good times and the bad times, in the easy times and the difficult times. I can choose to praise God. He commands me to do so; therefore, I can, with His help.

When you change your attitude to one of praise, I promise you, your outlook on life will change as well. I remember reading about two shoe salesmen that traveled by boat to a distant island to sell shoes. When they landed on a good-sized island and looked around, they found thousands and thousands of barefooted people. Both of the salesmen got right on the telephone.

The first salesman called his office and said, "Hey, boss, we came all this way for no good reason. No one here even wears shoes. I'm coming home."

The second salesman called the office and said, "Hey, boss, guess what? No one over here wears shoes! Send me 10,000 pairs. I've got a lot of customers!"

It's not the situation; it's your outlook that is important. When you see everything as something that God is using to make you more like Jesus, you can see it as a good thing—just as Romans 8:28 says it is—and you can praise Him for it.

You can look at your circumstances and see them as struggles or as opportunities. You must tell yourself at every turn, "It's my choice. I can see this as a real downer, or I can see this as an opportunity for God to show Himself strong in my life."

6. Develop a biblical perspective of God, understanding His mercy and His lovingkindness toward you.

You will not see your problems as problems when you realize that God has a wonderful plan for you to become more like His Son. He wants to salvage your broken life and fix it. He wants to change you into something beautiful so that He can use your life and bless it.

Your problems will not seem like problems when you understand that God is taking the bad things that Satan is using to destroy you and turning them into good things that He can use to build you.

Your problems will not seem like problems when you realize that God is wise and gives you exactly what you need but never more than you can handle. He is always with you to carry the heavy burdens and to pick you up when you fall.

Your problems will not seem like problems when you know He cares. He is listening with an attentive ear, and He is waiting anxiously with open arms any time you need some help.

Your problems will not seem like problems when you realize that God is bigger than any problem. Nothing is too hard for Him to handle.

How do you develop this biblical perspective of God? It will come as you get to know Him, as you spend time in His Word and on your knees in prayer, as you diligently seek His face. Get to know God; learn to love Him. I promise that as you turn your eyes upon Jesus, "the things of earth will grow strangely dim in the light of His glory and grace."

Conclusion

Problems beset us all, but negative thoughts and feelings do not change our problems or make them disappear. They only make matters worse. Rather than wallow in a past, dominated by gloom and despair, we must seek out the only lasting hope available. That hope is found in our wonderful God. Take your hands off the controls of your life and allow Him to do the work that only He can do—transforming your thinking and changing your heart. Seek Him diligently. Seek Him daily, and you will find Him to be an ever present help in time of need just as He promised. If you need help in finding your way back to God, seek some biblical counseling to give you some accountability and to help you get started on the right path. Take heart, friend. God wants to do a miraculous work in your heart. Let that work begin today.

4

When You Feel Like Quitting

GALATIANS 6:6–10

Let him that is taught in the word communicate unto him that teacheth in all good things. Be not deceived; God is not mocked: for whatsoever a man soweth, that shall he also reap. For he that soweth to his flesh shall of the flesh reap corruption; but he that soweth to the Spirit shall of the Spirit reap life everlasting. And let us not be weary in well doing: for in due season we shall reap, if we faint not. As we have therefore opportunity, let us do good unto all men, especially unto them who are of the household of faith.

There is one thing that is certain about life: it is full of disappointments, heartaches, turmoil, and frustrations. We all get worn down. That's just life. Without a doubt, there are times you want to quit—just give up and throw in the towel. I know I do at times, but we can find the fortitude to keep doing what is right! The Bible tells us how to persevere, even when we feel like giving up. I want you to look with me at a few verses from Paul's letter to the Galatians. There are some action points that we can draw from one basic principle—the principle of sowing and reaping.

It's All about Sowing and Reaping

In this particular passage, the sowing and reaping principle refers to giving, but it's a universal principle. Take notice of verse 7: "*Be not deceived; God is not mocked: for whatsoever a man soweth, that shall he also reap.*" He's giving us in that "whatsoever" a reference to any thought or attitude, action or habit we choose as "seed." This seed will germinate and bring forth its natural product. If I plant some tomato plants, I can expect to reap tomatoes from those plants. If I plant an apple seed, I can expect to see apples on the tree that springs up. If I don't sow apple seed, I'm not going to get apples. I will have to buy my apples at the grocery store. If I sow the seed, I will reap the fruit. If I don't, I won't. That's the sowing and reaping principle.

The principle is the same in the spiritual realm. If you're the sort of person that yells at your spouse and children, you're going to reap the undesirable consequences that come from that behavior. If you try to cheat the IRS and get away without paying your taxes, you can be confident that you will be haunted by that decision some day.

Along with the principle, God gives a promise in verse 9: "*And let us not be weary in well doing: for in due season we shall reap, if we faint not.*" So, if we simply do not allow ourselves to grow weary and quit, the Bible says we *shall* reap. There is a thought, a mindset actually, related to this principle. While you are waiting for the harvest from all the sowing you've been doing, there is never any good time to quit. It is important to have as our mindset the determination to continue sowing, even if the reaping seems very distant.

What Should We Be Sowing?

The Lord tells us that we should not grow weary in well doing. What is "well doing"? *Well doing is doing the will of God*, anything that God has set forth for my life, any responsibility He has given me, any job He has for me to do. As a Christian, I want to do the best I can at whatever it is God has given me. I believe that anyone who holds the name of Jesus Christ should certainly hold to a higher standard in his work—whatever it is—than someone who is not a Christian.

Well doing is also any good deed done in the name of Jesus Christ. Good deeds might entail maintaining a good testimony at work, living above reproach, or nurturing loving relationships with your family, friends and neighbors. It certainly means witnessing to others who need the Gospel.

The problem with "people work" is that it can be very discouraging. It is easy to give up on people when they are ungrateful or unresponsive or even downright belligerent. You may say, "Well, I've talked to my friend, neighbor, coworker, or family member about the Lord, but he has rejected it again and again. I'm ready to give up." Don't! Nothing else in this life really matters, because nothing else really matters to God. He loves people. Don't give up on them!

The action points I give here are some areas in which you may find yourself growing weary and wanting to throw in the towel, but God says, "Don't do it. Keep planting good seeds." If you continue faithfully sowing the right things, God will give you a harvest of good things.

ACTION POINT #1—CARE FOR YOUR MINISTERS

Galatians 6:6 says, "*Let him that is taught in the word communicate unto him that teacheth in all good things.*" Evidently some men in the church at Galatia had been teaching the Word of God as their life's calling. God admonished the people being helped by those teachers to take care of them. That's the precept: we are supposed to take care of those that teach us the Word of God. How is this supposed to be an encouragement to you when you feel overwhelmed by life and want to quit? I'm glad you asked! The principle of sowing and reaping applies here. Keep encouraging others, and God will send some encouragement your way.

ACTION POINT #2–TEACH YOUR CHILDREN THE WORD OF GOD

Another area that will reap great dividends is that of teaching your children the Word of God. Training children takes perseverance because you must constantly battle the child's inherent sinful nature. The Bible says, "*Foolishness is bound in the heart of the child*" (Proverbs 22:15). There will be struggles and difficulties as you instruct children in righteousness, but don't give up on them. Line upon line, precept upon precept, stay at the task of teaching all the time. The first and best opportunity for your children to learn about righteousness and the love of God is in your home. That, of course, assumes that you have a home where God is lifted up and His righteousness is exalted.

ACTION POINT #3–LOVE YOUR SPOUSE

Another struggle you may be facing is the temptation to stop loving your spouse. Most people come to a place where they doubt their relationship, wondering, "Is this worth it? It just isn't working out the way I thought it would." Soon, there is fussing and feuding between them. If you are there, you may think, "I'm about ready to quit. We're just not compatible. If I'd only known this before we got married!" Well, you didn't know, but you're married—'til death do you part. Now you need to focus on answers to your problems, and there *are* answers to any marital problem you might face. But before you will make any headway, you must commit to staying and working things out because good relationships don't just happen; they take work.

Temptation to Quit

There are several temptations that cause us to turn back from the well doing that God has planned for us to do.

THE FLESH

The number one culprit causing people to quit doing what they *should* be doing is doing what they *should not* be doing. For some, turning back to their fleshly ways may seem an easier path than battling the flesh, the world, and the devil every day. They have been taking one fiery dart after another, and when they are battle-scarred and weary, an imp from Hell will tell them they should surrender. He'll remind them of the good ol' days partying with friends. He'll tell them they can't understand the Bible and that following its precepts is oppressive. He'll promise them that life will be easier if they quit serving and they will have more money if they quit giving. He'll promise that they will be happier without their spouse and that their children will be okay if they leave. The devil will make all kinds of promises, and because the Christian life is not all roses, some people *will* quit and return to the path of least resistance—their flesh.

Before you choose that path, I would like you to consider what you are choosing. The Bible says that if you sow to the flesh, you shall *"of the flesh reap corruption."* You can take any sinful act and realize that if you continue in that sin, you can expect, as a result, to reap a harvest of corruption.

The specific sinful act does not matter; the principle remains true. Maybe you're not going to go back to partying with the guys. Maybe you'll just have a drink with the boss after work. If you keep drinking, you will get drunk. If you repeat this behavior enough, you will become a drunk. A drunk will have difficulties with even the routine affairs of living, and the more serious problems of life will overwhelm him.

It may not turn out that way at all for you. Maybe your child, who is following the example he sees, will become an alcoholic. Maybe you will lose your spouse. Maybe you will end up in jail because you killed someone while driving under the influence. All this may sound very negative, but my point is *you don't get to choose how you will reap*—and you will reap. If you sow to the flesh, sooner or later you *will* reap corruption.

God never promised that walking in the Spirit and serving Him would be easy. On the contrary, He tells us that following Him will mean bearing a cross. He does promise, however, that a spiritual life will be blessed—in this life and in the next. And unlike Satan who never keeps his promises, God does keep His promises and will send the harvest if you will be patient enough to wait for the reaping time. Friend, keep your eyes on the prize as the Apostle Paul did.

Think about the many different hardships Paul endured to do what God had called him to do. Try to visualize Paul shivering in a dank, dark prison cell, his rough clothing clinging to open wounds where flesh was ripped from his back, his head pounding and his body reeling from blood loss and hunger. Imagine his excruciating pain as he slowly regained consciousness and pulled his crushed body—bruised and bleeding—from a heap of stones meant to mark the grave of a despicable blasphemer. Envision Paul collapsing onto a sandy shore having spent the night in frigid, turbulent waves, pelted by wind and rain, as he clung desperately to wreckage from what had been the ship that would take him to another city to tell others about Christ. His strength completely spent, his body convulsing, he must have questioned, "Is obeying Christ worth all the hardship and suffering?"

What kept him from quitting? I believe that Paul looked up from that dirty cell, that pile of stones, that cold, wet sand and saw only one thing—His precious Saviour. He clung to the expectation that one day he would hear Jesus' voice saying, "Well done, Paul." Keeping his eyes focused on the prize is what sustained Paul through incomprehensible suffering. If Paul could finish his course, so can we.

DOING GOOD RATHER THAN BEST

Culprit number two, loss of perspective, is Satan's more subtle, and therefore more common, way to keep people from well doing. Maybe the devil cannot get you to quench the Holy Spirit with a six-pack of beer, but he might be able to get you sidetracked with thumbtacks and staples, and computers and documents so that you forget why you are doing what you are doing. God put you where you are because He has a job He wants you to do, and shuffling papers is not the primary reason He has you behind that desk. The people in the cubicles around you are your mission. Don't lose that perspective. Don't quit doing the job He has given you to do.

Satan's tactic of skewing our perspective is subtle for two reasons. We are so busy doing "good" things that we do not perceive our error. We may never ponder, "Am I doing the most important things?" Another subtlety of this tactic is that our behavior is easy to justify with reasoning that says, "I am not doing anything wrong; therefore, nothing needs to change." But if you are spinning your wheels doing what is right in your own eyes, you are not doing what God has planned for you.

Sin is not the only thing that besets us as Christians. Take some time to evaluate your life. Are you running the course God has set for you? The futility of doing good things rather than the best things can lead a person to feel unfulfilled and ready to quit.

SELF-SUFFICIENCY

Another culprit that brings us down—physical and spiritual weariness—is often the result of our own self-sufficiency. You need to read only a few accounts of the Israelites' battles to understand how God feels about our self–sufficiency. Samson is a prime example of one who had misplaced confidence.

Rather than raise up an army to defeat the Philistines, Israel's adversaries, God raised up one man, Samson, through whom He would display His amazing strength to deliver the Israelites. Having soundly defeated thousands of Philistines single-handedly, Samson must have become confident in his own abilities. He was sadly mistaken in thinking that his strength was of himself.

He divulged to Delilah, against the commandment of the Lord, that the secret of his strength was in his hair. Armed with this lethal information, she called for a man to shave off Samson's hair while he slept like a baby in her lap. When the Philistines came upon Samson *"he awoke out of his sleep, and said, I will go out as at other times before, and shake myself"* (Judges 16:20). In Jeremiah 17:5, God reveals His sentiment regarding this kind of trust in human ability: *"Thus saith the LORD; Cursed be the man that trusteth in man, and maketh flesh his arm, and whose heart departeth from the LORD."* Self-sufficiency is a sin.

Samson figured he would do what he had always done before, but this time was different. God was not with him, and he didn't even know it. The Bible says, *"And he wist not that the LORD was departed from him."*

The Christian life is a spiritual battle, and we can't go it alone. It requires us to be patient and to rely on the Lord. But our tendency is to take things into our own hands and to labor in our own strength as Samson tried to do.

The outcome of Gideon's battle was quite different from Samson's. God gave Gideon the assignment to wipe out the Midianites, but he would do this task with such a small band of men that there would be no doubt that God gave the victory. God told him, "I want you to circle the Midianite camp. Then, on the count of three (or however He said it!), I want your men to blow their trumpets so that it will sound like you have many squads of platoons coming into the camp. Then take clay pots or pitchers and smash them together to give out a great noise."

In the middle of the night they did just as God had told them. They blew their trumpets and smashed their pitchers. The Midianite camp woke up to all the clamor, thinking, "People are coming in from every side! They're going to wipe us out!" In the confusion and darkness, the Midianties turned on each other, and God gave Gideon's band a great victory. What an unusual battle. Not a bow was drawn nor a sword was pulled by God's righteous people to win this.

Gideon and his men trusted God to do the job they could not do with all their deficiencies, and so must we. We are not wise enough or strong enough to do God's work on our own. We cannot train children on our own. We cannot have a good marriage without God's help. We cannot win souls or edify God's people without supernatural power. When we try, we are just spinning our wheels. We put forth much effort, but accomplish little, and this self-effort causes the frustration and weariness that makes us want to give up. If you are feeling frustrated and defeated, it may be because you are trying to handle things without God's Word and prayer, without seeking God's wisdom and guidance, without relying on His power and strength.

Life Is All about Making Choices

Whether a Christian turns back to a sinful life, chooses to do good things over the best things, or simply burns out in self-effort and gives up, his regression is based on choices. No one just "falls into sin" as we often hear people say, as if the fault is excused. We walk into sin. It's a choice.

I don't have to yell at my spouse. I can yield myself to the Spirit's control. I don't have to neglect my Bible reading because I have paperwork to catch up on. I can do the spiritual things first. I don't have to rely on my own strength for my Christian service. I can rely on God's strength and wisdom to get the job done.

I'm simply saying God does not leave us without choices. We may feel at times that we have no options, but that's not true. God always lets us do what we choose to do.

Though we do have choices, the decision-making process is swayed by the influences we allow to affect our thinking. What influences in your life are discouraging you to the point that you want to quit?

NEGATIVE PEOPLE

Negative, complaining people can have a powerful influence on the way we think. A friendship in which your conversations often involve murmuring and complaining—you were treated wrongly, you didn't get what you deserved, some other guy got what he didn't deserve, the boss made a bad decision, and on and on it could go—isn't the kind of friendship that encourages. If you can't turn the conversations you have with certain people toward a positive, godly tone, I suggest you limit the time you spend with them to only that which is unavoidable.

WORLDLY INFLUENCES

Also, be careful about the influence you allow this world to have on you. The devil has designed an entire world system to condition, even manipulate, our thinking. The world will tell you all sorts of nonsense: "Just do it," "Go for the gusto," "You deserve a break today." These philosophies will dictate our values and priorities, our attitudes and opinions, our reasoning and perspective, and ultimately our actions. God tells us in Proverbs 4:23, with very good reason, that we must guard our hearts: *"Keep thy heart with all diligence; for out of it are the issues of life."* What we allow to enter our hearts will determine how our lives are lived; therefore, it is of the utmost importance that we take heed to guard our hearts. Remember, we are to be in the world, but not of the world.

NEGATIVE THOUGHTS

Without a doubt, people impact us and the world pressures us, but sometimes our own negative introspection is the problem when we feel like quitting. We are sinful creatures; therefore, unannounced, negative thoughts will drop by at times—no doubt with an armload of paraphernalia to throw a pity party—but we do not have to welcome them in and entertain them. When they show up at *your* door, don't answer it. Nip that visit in the bud!

The Bible tells you in 2 Corinthians 10:5 to take your thoughts into captivity, but if you choose to dwell on thoughts that are dragging you down to a deeper state of despondency, you are not controlling your thoughts; they are controlling you.

The first decision you must make is what you will allow to influence your heart. We can and must choose what we allow to affect us, for those influences will sway all the other decisions we make. It will take determination and effort to change our behavior, but it is essential to continuing steadfastly as the Bible instructs us.

ACTION POINT #4—MAKE THE CHOICE TO PERSEVERE

If you will persevere, if you will continue in well doing, you must determine to do so. Before your child becomes a teenager and tests your limits, decide you will hold to your standards. Before financial crisis comes, decide if you will keep giving. Before leadership disappoints you, decide you will stay in church. Before difficulties and hardships come, decide you will continue in well doing. When burdens come, that is not the time to make life-altering decisions. Hold on, and determine to do right no matter what.

We base all of our choices on what we value most. Therefore, we must value those things that God values. We must develop the mind of Christ. Romans 12:2 says it this way: *"And be not conformed to this world: but be ye transformed by the renewing of your mind, that ye may prove what is that good, and acceptable, and perfect, will of God."* A renewed mind is the only thing that will transform a life.

Quitting Begins in Your Mind

If you are prone to negative thinking, you are definitely at risk for quitting because that's where the weariness and despondency that causes us to quit begins—in the mind. The Bible bears that out in Hebrews 12:3: *"For consider him that endured such contradiction of sinners against himself, lest ye be wearied and faint in your minds."*

In the same chapter, the Bible gives us some very good instruction on how to change our thinking when we feel like quitting. It tells us where to place our focus when we want to give up. The writer said, "When you are weary and ready to give up, think about the Lord Jesus Christ for a moment." Think about the Son of God who humbled Himself to take on human flesh, with all of its infirmities, so that He could empathize with our frailties. Think about what He experienced—hunger, cold, pain, and grief. Yet not much comfort was afforded Him. As He walked this sod, He had not so much as a place to lay His head. He endured overwhelming temptation so that He could be touched with the feelings of our infirmities. The exalted Prince of Heaven stooped to become one of us.

If that were not enough, He endured lies and betrayal and rejection. He took spitting and mocking, buffeting and scourging. He traded His royal diadem for a crown of thorns, His royal scepter for an instrument of torture. Worse yet, the holy Prince of Heaven became sin. Every wicked device, every perverted thought, every disgusting deed conceived by mankind was laid on Him. He stomached the shame and the guilt. Even His Father had to turn His back on the repulsive sight. Yet, knowing what He would suffer, Jesus set His face like a flint and submitted Himself to the howling mob and the ruthless executioners. He did it for you and for me with a heart full of love. He stayed with it until He finished what He came to do—redeem mankind. The Lord endured strong opposition from sinful men (the seed sown) to make salvation possible for all of mankind (the harvest reaped).

Consider the example you see in the life of Jesus. Before you give up, set your face like a flint and decide this: I will finish what God has called me to do. I will not give up. I will not give in.

Now consider your own life. Hebrews 12:4 tells us, "*Ye have not resisted unto blood...*" as Jesus did. Very few, if any of us, have shed blood for our faith. We have not endured anything close to what Jesus endured for us. So when you feel like you have suffered more than you can bear, consider Jesus. Your trials will not seem so hard, your burdens so heavy. The time of reaping is at hand. Don't give up just short of the harvest.

ACTION POINT #5—DEVELOP GODLY THINKING

If you grow weary in your mind, you are as good as done. But consider this: if it is in your mind that you will be defeated, it is also in your mind that you will have victory. Therefore, your responsibility—and the first and best defense against feelings of defeat—is to give your mind over to God to be renewed and refreshed.

As I mentioned before, it's up to each one of us to cast out negative thoughts, but we must also replace them with proper thoughts. What does God want us to think on? He tells us in Philippians 4:8: *"Finally, brethren, whatsoever things are true, whatsoever things are honest, whatsoever things are just, whatsoever things are pure, whatsoever things are lovely, whatsoever things are of good report; if there be any virtue, and if there be any praise, think on these things."* If we will focus our thoughts only on things that have virtue and praise, we will develop a proper, godly perspective.

Is your glass half full or half empty? You can focus on the empty part of the glass, on all the things you lack—the unmet expectations, the frustrated goals, the shattered dreams. Or you can choose to focus on the abundant blessings that your glass holds. If the only thing you can find to be thankful for is a God who loved you enough to sacrifice His Son so that you could be forgiven of all your sins, you have more than anyone deserves. You are blessed above measure! If you will focus your eyes on His goodness every day, you will see that every day is a miracle—a gift from God. With a proper perspective you will see how big your God really is.

Can you imagine how big God is? Scientists have recently discovered a new star with a diameter that is three times the distance between the earth and our sun—93 million miles. It takes a big God to fling a star 279 million miles in diameter into the sky, but that's our God, the God of the universe. That's the God who created you and me.

"Hast thou not known? hast thou not heard, that the everlasting God, the LORD, the Creator of the ends of the earth, fainteth not, neither is weary? there is no searching of his understanding" (Isaiah 40:28). God never wears

out. He never gets weary. His strength and power are available to you if you will rely on Him for them. Verse 29 says, *"He giveth power to the faint; and to them that have no might he increaseth strength."* Hey look, when you're trying to get to the finish line as you run your course for God, He'll increase your strength. At those times that you feel like quitting because you're short on strength, turn to God. He will give you might. *"Even the youths shall faint and be weary, and the young men shall utterly fall: But they that wait upon the LORD shall renew their strength; they shall mount up with wings as eagles; they shall run, and not be weary; and they shall walk, and not faint"* (Isaiah 40:30–31).

Verse 31 is a wonderful promise to us! Look to Jesus Christ, and He will give you strength. When you think, "I can't take my spouse any longer," look to Jesus. When you think, "I've had it with this job. I can't take the constant pressures and the problems," look to Jesus. No matter what weighs you down, look to Jesus for help.

ACTION POINT #6—HAVE DAILY PRAYER

One of the first steps downward in a Christian's life is when he quits having devotions. In Luke 18:1 the Bible says, *"And he* [Jesus] *spake a parable unto them to this end, that men ought always to pray, and not to faint."* Praying is hard work. It's difficult, but God says men should always pray rather than faint or give up.

You may say, "But I get tired when I pray." Hey, guess what? I do, too! That's the main reason I walk every morning. It's not for the exercise—that's the second reason. The first reason is to pray. Don't stop praying.

Think about what you will miss if you stop praying. You will not have the help, strength, wisdom, and guidance you need from that very big God that we just talked about.

ACTION POINT #7—LEARN YOUR BIBLE

Bible reading is just as important to our spiritual lives. We must have the infusion of the Word of God coming into our lives. A person who doesn't read his Bible every day is headed for destruction.

A mind that is renewed and a life that is transformed is one that is full of the Bible. Colossians 3:16 admonishes us, *"Let the word of Christ dwell in you richly in all wisdom...."* The Word of God will not dwell in you richly if you read a thought for the day or check off a few verses on a schedule. You must come to the Word of God looking for Him, seeking His face, longing to hear from Him. Read God's Word. Study it. Memorize it. Meditate on it. When you do, your mind will be renewed. You won't struggle so much with negative thoughts because your problems will take on a whole new light. You will see them as appointments from God, not burdens to escape. You will find the peace that passes understanding because you will know the God of peace.

You may say, "Well, I've tried reading the Bible and I just don't get much out of it." That's for one of two reasons:

1. You're not a Christian. You may think you are. You may be religious, you may have joined a church, you may have been baptized, but this doesn't mean you have been born again into God's family. One evidence of the new birth is that your life has been changed by the Holy Spirit of God. So, if you haven't had Him change your life, if you do not desire the things of God, make sure of your salvation. (See page 193 for God's instruction about how to be born again.)

2. You find it hard to understand. So you've given up. Though it may be difficult to understand at first, if you stay with it you'll begin to understand. It's no different from when you started any subject in school. You may have thumbed through the book on the first day and thought, "I don't even understand what they are saying." But through perseverance and some instruction from a good teacher you began to understand little by little.

If you will persevere at your Bible study and ask your Teacher, the Holy Spirit, to help you, you will be amazed at how clear it becomes.

ACTION POINT #8—REALIZE YOUR PROBLEMS COME TO STRENGTHEN YOUR FAITH

The devil sometimes brings problems into a Christian's life to destroy him. Such was the case with Job, a mature and upright man. The devil did his best to make Job curse God to His face. He took everything Job had—his children, his prosperity, his health—everything.

But God had a different plan for those hardships. He used them to refine Job, to make him an even better man. That's what God does with our trials as well. *"For our light affliction, which is but for a moment, worketh for us a far more exceeding and eternal weight of glory"* (2 Corinthians 4:17). Job revealed his godly perspective on his trials in Job 23:10 when he said, *"But he knoweth the way that I take: when he hath tried me, I shall come forth as gold."* How did Job know God and trust Him so fully? This kind of trust, even in the face of hardships, comes from walking with Him daily.

You Can't Just Run Away

We grow weak and weary when we're faced with difficulties. The Bible says in Proverbs 24:10, *"If thou faint in the day of adversity, thy strength is small."* Do you have any adversities or afflictions in your life? In the face of these things, some of us will give up, and some of us will continue on. When the prophet Jonah was faced with a situation he didn't sign up for, he ran.

God said to Jonah, "I want you to go to Nineveh and preach the Word of God."

Jonah began reasoning, "Well, that isn't going to work out. If I preach to our enemies, the Ninevites, they're liable to run me out of town or, worse yet, stone me. I don't want to go there to preach to those wicked people." And Jonah didn't.

He decided to run instead. He jumped aboard a ship to Tarshish to flee *"from the presence of the Lord."* Then God sent a great wind and a mighty tempest in the sea. It was bad! Everybody was bailing water and throwing things overboard, but Jonah was fast asleep in the side of the ship. The shipmaster yelled at him, "Hey, wake up and call on your God. Maybe He will help us!"

The situation was getting so bad that they decided to find out who had caused this evil to come upon them. They drew straws and Jonah came up with the short end of the stick. They began to fire questions at Jonah: "What do you do? Where are you from? Who are your people?"

Jonah told them, "Fellows, I'm running from the God who made the sea and dry land. I'm your problem. The best thing to do is throw me overboard."

Instead they worked harder to bring the ship to dry land, but when they couldn't, they tossed Jonah into the raging sea.

God had already prepared a great fish to swallow Jonah when he hit that water. Can you imagine being inside that fish? Jonah sat there in seaweed and fish food because he had decided, "I'm going to quit. I don't need to do the things that God wants me to do. I'll run my life myself." That's just the way we think when we are tempted to quit. "I've tried to live for God at work, but it's not working. I have all these trials, and I'm weak, and I'm just going to live like I want to live." You may be tempted to quit your service to God, or to quit your marriage, but don't do it. Don't grow weary in well doing.

It may be that you're tempted to quit managing your financial obligations. Your debt is running high, and your plastic can't extend any further. Bill collectors are calling, and when the struggle to pay these obligations just seems too much to bear, you think, "What's the use?" Don't run from your financial pressures. You are responsible to pay off every nickel you owe. You can't amass a great pile of debt and just walk away from it. You have to say, "I have a responsibility here. I got myself into debt. I've got to get myself out of debt." But, don't quit, and don't take the easy way out. Bring these responsibilities before God and ask Him for wisdom.

If you think you can run away from problems, you're wrong. God does not let "Jonahs" run. He brings them back! It's better to face your problems with God than to run away from the one who can help you. The easy way out is not always the easy way, as we saw in Jonah's life.

ACTION POINT #8–DON'T QUIT DOING WHAT'S RIGHT

I came across the following anonymous poem:

> When things go wrong as they sometimes will,
> When the road you're trudging seems all uphill,
> When the funds are low and the debts are high,
> And you want to smile but you have to sigh,
> When cares are pressing you down a bit,
> Rest if you must, but don't you quit.
>
> Life is weird with its twist and turns,
> As every one of us sometimes learns,
> And many a failure turns about
> When he might have won had he stuck it out.
>
> Don't give up, though the pace seems slow,
> You may succeed with another blow.
> Often the goal is nearer than it seems
> To a faint and a faltering man.
>
> Often the struggler has given up
> When he might have captured the victor's cup,
> And he learned too late when the night slipped down
> How close he was to the golden crown.
>
> Success is failure turned inside out,
> The silver tint of the clouds of doubt.
> And you can never tell how close you are,
> It may be near when it seems afar,
> So stick to the fight when you're hardest hit.
> It's when things seem worse that you mustn't quit.

Remember the promise. If we don't grow weary in well doing, we shall reap. It is a guaranteed promise of God that if I stay true to the task and fulfill my God-given responsibilities, God will bless me. I will reap. It's harvest time when the struggling is done.

Quitting Is an Attitude

Check your attitude. If you think you are defeated, you're right. If you think that you have the ability to keep going, you're right. Many people become quitters and failures because of their attitudes. This should not be so of a Christian. We must believe that if we won't give up, that if we'll learn to trust God with our circumstances, He knows exactly when to end the race for you and for me. So let's not quit ahead of time. Instead, we must develop the right attitude, an attitude of explicit trust in Jesus Christ.

The right attitude will see you through the really difficult times; the wrong attitude will sink you, as was the case with the two frogs that fell into the can of cream. The sides of the can were shiny and steep. The cream was deep and cold. "We can't climb out, and we have no one to help us, so what's the use," croaked number one. "It's fate. Goodbye, cruel world." And still weeping, he drowned.

But frog number two was made of sterner stuff. This frog paddled in surprise at his predicament. "I'll swim awhile, at least," he thought. For an hour or two he kicked and swam. Not once did he stop to mutter or complain. Kicking and kicking and paddling and kicking. Finally, exhausted and emotionally spent, frog number two—barely able to get any spring into his weary leg—hopped out by standing on top of the can of...butter. The frog's hard work and positive attitude paid off in the end, and so will yours if you just keep paddling. If you need help from someone else, get it. If you need counsel, get it; pour out your heart to God, but don't give up.

When the Apostle Paul began his first missionary journey, he took several friends with him. Among the group were Barnabas, and

Barnabas's relative John Mark (the same John Mark, experts say, who wrote the gospel of Saint Mark in our Bible). Some persecution arose along the way, and the Bible, in Acts 13, says that John Mark departed—he threw in the towel. But later on, John Mark came back and tried to pick up where he left off. Good for John Mark! He changed his attitude. He picked himself up after disappointment and prepared himself again to engage in the work.

Paul and Barnabas parted ways because of the situation, but John Mark joined Barnabas on his missionary journey and obviously became a great man, used of God to record the Gospel that bears his name. Later Paul described John Mark as profitable to him for the ministry. He had been a quitter, but he got up and shook it off. The circumstances did not get any easier. The only thing that changed was John Mark's attitude. Quitting is an attitude.

It may be that you have already quit. Perhaps you should say, "I need to be like John Mark. I need to get back in the race and start giving my very best to the Lord."

Some Final Things to Consider

If you are not sure that you are a Christian, consider these things.

If you want to be defeated, look back. If you want to be distracted, look around. If you want to be dismayed, look within. But if you want to be delivered, look up. The time for your salvation is now. The Bible says, *"And the LORD said, My Spirit shall not always strive with man…"* (Genesis 6:3). The Bible describes God as longsuffering and kind. He's a God of second chances, and third and fourth and tenth and hundreds of chances! But there *will* come an end to God's waiting. Someday God may quit seeking your soul, and it's going to be your fault. Don't wait to repent. Don't quit in your search for God. Don't give up the hope that there is something better.

If you haven't been saved, give God the opportunity to save your soul and to transform your life. Just say, "Lord, I'm not running away from You any longer." If you are serious in your search for God, He will give you the opportunity to be saved. He will give you new hope and new purpose.

Once you are saved, get going for God. Start serving Him and decide to keep on going for Him. Don't ever even think about quitting.

5

When You Feel You Missed God's Purpose for Your Life

I'm going to tell you a *big* fish story. I'm sure most of you have heard it before. But, just in case this story is new to you, I remind you, it is from God's Holy Word. I'm not making up any of it. I admit up front that parts of this story sound unusual, but it is true because it's right from God's Word.

JONAH 1:12–17

And he said unto them, Take me up, and cast me forth into the sea; so shall the sea be calm unto you: for I know that for my sake this great tempest is upon you. Nevertheless the men rowed hard to bring it to the land; but they could not: for the sea wrought, and was tempestuous against them. Wherefore they cried unto the LORD, and said, We beseech thee, O LORD, we beseech thee, let us not perish for this man's life, and lay not upon us innocent blood: for thou, O LORD, hast done as it pleased thee. So they took up Jonah, and cast him forth into the sea: and the sea ceased from her raging. Then the men feared the LORD exceedingly, and offered a sacrifice unto the

LORD, and made vows. Now the LORD had prepared a great fish to swallow up Jonah. And Jonah was in the belly of the fish three days and three nights.

Knowing God's Will for Your Life

God has a perfect will for your life just as He has for mine. There is not anyone for whom God has not planned out a specific will. It's not a matter of whether God has something for you to do, but whether you are doing it. If your response is, "I don't even know what God's will is for my life," then I can tell you with some confidence that you're not doing the will of God.

If you feel unfulfilled and disillusioned with life, it may be because you are missing out on God's best for you, but that doesn't have to be the end of your story. Read the last line in Paul's salutation to the church of Colossae: "*...that ye may stand perfect and complete in all the will of God*" (Colossians 4:12). He told the Colossians, "This is my prayer for you, that you would be perfect and complete in the will of God." This is my prayer for you as well.

As you read this chapter and meditate on the Word of God, I desire that God will show you how to stand perfect and complete in His will for your life, for He has made His will very plain. If you read carefully and seriously, you will gain some enlightenment that can help you better discern the specific will of God for your life.

How God Communicates His Will to Man

Jonah was a Jew with a great disdain for Gentiles (anyone who was not a Jew). But God had a job for Jonah to do—preach to these Gentile people. "*Now the word of the LORD came unto Jonah the son of Amittai, saying,*

Arise, go to Nineveh, that great city, and cry against it; for their wickedness is come up before me" (Jonah 1:1–2).

God communicated His specific will to Jonah. Notice how He did that. "*Now the word of the LORD came unto Jonah....*" That is precisely the same way He communicates His will to us—through the Word of the Lord, the Bible. My guess is that approximately 95% of God's will for our lives comes this way, directly from the Bible. Most of the other 5% comes as the Holy Spirit guides each individual Christian. That is, God the Holy Spirit impresses our hearts with specifics that apply to our own lives as we study the Bible.

He uses the Bible stories and the lives of the characters and the letters to Christian churches to show me His mind on matters. He gives me specific commandments and teaches me principles for living. God's Holy Spirit speaks to me through the Word of God as I read it and study it and as I hear it in church services. Through the Word of God, the Holy Spirit moves on my heart and helps me know exactly what it is that God has in mind for me. If you are not reading and hearing the Word of God, you will remain ignorant of God's particular will for you.

God used His Word to give Jonah his marching orders: "*Arise, go to Nineveh, that great city, and cry against it; for their wickedness is come up before me*" (Jonah 1:2). He was told that it was time to get up, get going, and go to Nineveh, the capital of Assyria, an ancient power. It has been estimated that there were well over 600,000 people in Nineveh at the time, and God wanted these people to be warned about the impending judgment for their wickedness. Time was running out for them, and He wanted Jonah to go tell them.

God gave this specific direction to Jonah, but he refused. "*But Jonah rose up to flee unto Tarshish from the presence of the LORD, and went down to Joppa; and he found a ship going to Tarshish: so he paid the fare thereof, and went down into it, to go with them unto Tarshish from the presence of the LORD*" (Jonah 1:3). Jonah didn't like the will of God for his life; it was that simple.

Jonah Thought He Could Run

I imagine God must have shaken His head when He looked at Jonah. He actually believed that he could run from the presence of the Lord, and he certainly did try. God wanted him to go to Nineveh about 125 miles away in a northeasterly direction. Instead, Jonah, said, "I'm getting out of here!" He got on a ship to sail due west to Tarshish—2,500 miles in the opposite direction from where God wanted him to go.

As we look at Jonah, we think, "This is crazy." It does seem ridiculous that someone would try to escape God's notice, but I've been there. I have thought, "I can hide. I can do this, and no one will find out." We *all* think that way at times, and it's just as foolish when we play the game Jonah played.

Why was Jonah so resolute that he would get on a ship and travel nearly 2,500 miles? The truth of the matter is, as we see later in chapter 4, Jonah really didn't want to warn the Ninevites of their impending judgment because He knew that they would probably repent, and God, being abundantly gracious, would pour out His mercy on those wicked and vicious people.

In reality, he was saying, "I'm a Jew, and I don't care about those dirty Gentiles." In today's terminology we might say something like this: "I hate that guy at work. He has made my life miserable, and I don't care if he never gets saved. He will get what he deserves!"

Do you ever find yourself thinking like Jonah? Do you ever find yourself scheming like Jonah? He had his plan. He went down to Joppa, found a ship, paid his fare, and said, "I'm heading out of town. If someone is going to Nineveh, it's not going to be me!" Be warned up front about this matter. Whatever your reasons, you're facing a losing battle if you think you can design your own scheme and everything will turn out just the way you planned it. Sure, God let Jonah plunk down his money and get on that ship. It was smooth sailing for a while. In fact, Jonah was so confident his plan was working out that he went down into the ship, found a comfortable spot, and slept like a rock. But then all his plans went south.

You Can't Run Away from the Sight of God

Notice Jonah 1:3 starts out, "*But Jonah....*" By contrast, verse 4 begins, "*But the LORD....*" When you have two strong wills, and one of those belongs to God, which one do you think will win?

Jonah said, "I'm not going to Nineveh! Let them all die in their sins. I don't care." So he jumped on board and sailed off. Everything was going fine for a while. "*But the LORD sent out a great wind into the sea, and there was a mighty tempest in the sea, so that the ship was like to be broken*" (Jonah 1:4).

The sailors on this ship were experienced seamen. They knew what they were doing, but when this tempest came, they were being thrown to and fro like nothing they had ever seen before, and they were scared to death. They even got religious and began crying to their gods. Look how the Bible describes them by verse 10. "*Then were the men exceedingly afraid, and said unto him* [Jonah], *Why hast thou done this? For the men knew that he fled from the presence of the LORD, because he had told them*" (Jonah 1:10).

One of the worst things that ever happened to me was the boat ride the government provided to transport me back home from Italy after I had served three years in the U.S. Army. Trust me, we're not talking about the Carnival Cruise ship here. We hit a storm, right in the middle of the Atlantic—nothing but water as far as the eye could see. This was in January, mind you, and it was cold! That troop carrier with about 1,800 passengers on board came up out of the water and crashed back down so hard my teeth shook. Over and over that ship reeled and jolted. It was a cruel and unusual punishment for a soldier who had been serving his country!

Being in a boat in the middle of the sea when a storm comes is a frightful experience to a novice, but here, in this story about Jonah, even the experienced sailors felt terrified. They worked franticly to bring the boat to land, but they were struggling against a force too great for them. Realizing they had no other option, they cast Jonah overboard as he had urged them to do in the first place.

Notice how God had been at work in all of this. He sent a great wind and a great fear; then He sent a great fish. *"Now the LORD had prepared a great fish to swallow up Jonah. And Jonah was in the belly of the fish three days and three nights"* (Jonah 1:17). God had to go to great measures to foil Jonah's plans. Plan A, taking a ship to Tarshish, had not worked out for him. So Jonah decided to try Plan B, drowning in the sea. God said, "No, Jonah, that plan is not going to work either. I already have an enormous fish here that I have prepared especially for you."

You may look at that story and wonder, "Is it really possible that Jonah could have been swallowed by a big fish? After all, wouldn't the stomach acids have eaten him up?" No, not when God prepares the fish. And that's what the Bible says: *"the LORD had prepared a great fish."*

God did a miraculous work to bring Jonah back into His will, and He will work relentlessly to bring you back to a place of blessing as well. He is already preparing whatever He deems necessary to bring you back because He is not willing to let you go—He loves you that much. It might be smooth sailing for you right now, but God will rock the boat sooner or later, *if* you are truly His child.

Jonah's Repentance

"Then Jonah prayed unto the LORD his God out of the fish's belly, And said, I cried by reason of mine affliction unto the LORD, and he heard me; out of the belly of hell cried I, and thou heardest my voice. For thou hadst cast me into the deep, in the midst of the seas; and the floods compassed me about: all thy billows and thy waves passed over me. Then I said, I am cast out of thy

sight; yet I will look again toward thy holy temple. The waters compassed me about, even to the soul: the depth closed me round about, the weeds were wrapped about my head. I went down to the bottoms of the mountains; the earth with her bars was about me for ever: yet hast thou brought up my life from corruption, O LORD my God. When my soul fainted within me I remembered the LORD: and my prayer came in unto thee, into thine holy temple. They that observe lying vanities forsake their own mercy. But I will sacrifice unto thee with the voice of thanksgiving; I will pay that that I have vowed. Salvation is of the LORD. And the LORD spake unto the fish, and it vomited out Jonah upon the dry land" (Jonah 2:1–10).

No question about it, Jonah recognized the fact that he had missed God's will. He had said no to God, and now he found himself entombed in the "belly of hell," entrapped within the bars of a self-inflicted prison cell. As he groped to untangle the weeds that strangled him, he realized what was happening. He was trapped within a beast that was diving deeper and deeper "to the bottom of the mountains," and that's when terror struck his heart. He felt the waters closing in upon him, "even to the soul," and he thought it would be "forever." There was no way out of his desperate situation. He waited in agony for death to come, but it was too slow and too painful. His soul fainted within him. That's when, the Bible tells us, he "*remembered the LORD*."

Jonah knew that God was there, but it took him three days in the tomb of corruption to come to himself and give up his own selfish will. When his pride was finally crushed, He cried out to the LORD his God.

Maybe your situation is not quite as dramatic as Jonah's. Maybe God is simply saying to you, "Be careful. Be careful about your dating; you're headed the wrong direction. Be careful about your marriage; you're stepping into dangerous territory. Be careful about your job; that's not the way I want you to handle that situation. Be careful." You may be thinking, "It's not a big deal—this little move I am planning won't change my relationship with God." Be careful. God has a specific plan to bless your life, and walking away from God's blessing *is* a big deal!

Jonah knew he had missed the will of God, and that's when he decided to straighten out some things. Notice what Jonah did to get back into the will of God. First, he had to recognize God's supremacy in his life. Jonah thought he had everything under control, but in the fish's belly, he had to humbly concede that God was in control. I am struck by Jonah's language as he acknowledges God: *"all thy billows and thy waves passed over me."* Jonah realized that God had been at work in his life. He said, *"For thou hadst cast me into the deep, in the midst of the seas."* Wait a minute; the Bible said the distraught sailors threw him overboard. But as Jonah recounts the story, he recognizes that God's all-powerful hand was in it.

Next, Jonah had to humbly repent. *"Then Jonah prayed unto the LORD his God out of the fish's belly, And said, I cried by reason of mine affliction unto the LORD, and he heard me; out of the belly of hell cried I, and thou heardest my voice"* (Jonah 2:1–2). Jonah cried out to God, and the Bible says that the Lord heard his cry because it came from a repentant heart. *"The sacrifices of God are a broken spirit: a broken and a contrite heart, O God, thou wilt not despise"* (Psalm 51:17). God anxiously awaits the cry of the contrite heart. He is ready to help His penitent child.

Finally, Jonah arrived at an attitude of surrender. He said, *"I will pay that that I have vowed."* The moment Jonah humbled himself to follow God's leading, God said the word, and the fish delivered the penitent preacher safely to dry land.

If you are out of God's will, God is waiting for you to acknowledge Him, repent of your sin, and surrender to His will. You don't want to wait until it's too late to turn back.

I was a student at East Carolina University in Greenville, NC, before I became a Christian. During the first summer break, I got saved. When I returned to the campus in the fall, I looked for opportunities to witness. One day, I rounded up a friend of mine, and the two of us spent the entire day on campus passing out 2,000 Gospel tracts to the students. I had a burden for them. So I was witnessing and learning as I went along.

One evening, I went off campus to a little coffee shop downtown to get a snack after studying. I spotted a forlorn looking man sitting at the counter and decided to sit beside him to engage him in conversation. We touched on various subjects, but then I got around to talking about the Lord, and I shared God's plan of salvation. When I got finished, I gave him a tract. He looked so pitifully sad as he said, "Young man, I *am* a Christian" (though I would not have guessed it).

He told me his story: "When I was a little boy, I accepted Jesus Christ as my Saviour; but when I became a teenager, I knew God had called me to be a preacher. I knew it clearly, but I didn't want to do it. So I fought it. Thinking I could run from God, I left that burden that God had put on my heart. I never went into the ministry. In fact, ultimately, I quit church altogether." He continued, "I've lost my job. I've lost my family." I knew he had lost his self-respect as well.

"Wow," I thought, "what a price to pay for running from God."

I gave the man a tract and talked to him about the Lord. I don't think I made an impact on his life; he, however, made an impact on mine. I'll never forget seeing what happens to a person who knowingly rejects God's will.

That's not where you want to find yourself, friend. If you are not doing God's will, I urge you to begin seeking it today.

GOD'S SPECIFIC WILL IS DIFFERENT FOR EACH OF US

God has a perfect will for you. It is not God's will for everyone to go into full-time ministry. God's will is different for each of us. He may want you to be in the ministry. He may want you to be in government. He may want you to be a computer programmer. He may want you to be a truck driver. He may want you to be a secretary or a schoolteacher or any number of things. God has a perfect will for everyone's life; it's up to each one of us to find God's specific will for our lives.

GOD'S GENERAL WILL IS THE SAME FOR EACH OF US

God has laid out some particulars that are His will for every one of us, regardless of gender, ethnicity, social class, or religion. Each of us is responsible to read God's Word and seek His will for our lives.

SALVATION IS GOD'S WILL

God has a will for your soul. "*The Lord is...not willing that any should perish, but that all should come to repentance*" (2 Peter 3:9). Clearly, it is God's will for you and for me to accept Jesus Christ as our Saviour to avoid the wrath of God and His severe judgment of sin.

"*And this is his commandment....*" What is God's commandment to us? Here it is: "*That we should believe on the name of his Son Jesus Christ, and love one another, as he gave us commandment*" (1 John 3:23). God cares for you so much that His greatest desire is to see you saved. He sacrificed His Son so that you and I could be saved. There is no more to discuss regarding God's will if you have not yet accepted Christ as your own personal Saviour. It is the starting point. (See more about accepting God's gift of salvation on page 195.)

A HOLY LIFE IS GOD'S WILL

The Bible says that a person who has accepted Jesus Christ as Saviour "*no longer should live the rest of his time in the flesh to the lusts of men, but to the will of God*" (1 Peter 4:2). Once you are saved God wants you to live the rest of your life in His will.

You might be thinking, "There was a time that I truly repented of my sin and asked Jesus to be my Saviour, but I'm out of the will of God," That may be true, but by the end of this chapter, with God's help, you can change that.

When you were born again, you became a member of God's family, and just as the parents of a child work to teach their child how to live, God also teaches His child how to live. How does He want you to live?

His will is that your life would be holy, which involves your morals, your values, and your priorities in life. Through His Word, the Bible, He teaches His children how to live. That's why He said, *"And be not conformed to this world: but be ye transformed by the renewing of your mind, that ye may prove what is that good, and acceptable, and perfect, will of God"* (Romans 12:2).

He is saying, "Don't get your moral values from the newspaper, television, or the people around you at work." Get your values from the Word of God. As believers, we are not to be conformed to this world. The world and society as we know them should not be the mold into which we Christians try to fit. Those of us who have put our faith in Jesus Christ get our marching orders from Heaven. We are to say, "All right, Lord, I'm not going to do what everyone else is doing just because they're doing it. I will go to the Bible to find out how You want me to live."

A THANKFUL HEART IS GOD'S WILL

One lesson that Jonah—and others who have returned to God—learned is thankfulness. Jonah probably thought, "If God is merciful to deliver me from this vile dungeon, I will thank Him for everything that comes my way—good or bad. I have been an ungrateful wretch."

The Bible says, *"In every thing give thanks: for this is the will of God in Christ Jesus concerning you"* (1 Thessalonians 5:18). Thankfulness is a must in order to be in the will of God. The believer who is walking with God will rejoice even in his problems and afflictions because he knows that everything that comes into his life is allowed by God to serve a purpose in making him more like Christ. He has learned to be content in Christ alone. Anything he receives above and beyond is a blessing.

The truth is that God does bless us abundantly. *"Blessed be the Lord, who daily loadeth us with benefits, even the God of our salvation. Selah"* (Psalm 68:19). We should develop an attitude that says, "I can thank God for everything He sees fit to bring into my life."

This life is too short to walk around with our heads hanging down. "I didn't get that promotion." "My car had a flat tire." "My home life is tough." There's not enough time to dwell on those things when you have so many blessings to count. Learn to rejoice. Learn to be thankful. Jonah did. So can you.

GIVING OF YOURSELF IS GOD'S WILL

Second Corinthians 8:5 says, *"And this they did, not as we hoped, but first gave their own selves to the Lord, and unto us by the will of God."* This verse holds two key characteristics of a person in the will of God. You see those people, first of all, actively serving God and loving Him. And second, they give themselves to others to serve them. That is what the Christian life is all about.

In John 21, when Jesus asked Peter three times, *"Simon, son of Jonas, lovest thou me?"* Peter finally answered, *"Lord, thou knowest all things; thou knowest that I love thee."* Essentially Jesus told him to prove it when He said, *"Feed my sheep."*

If I love God, it will result in my giving myself to others, serving others. You say, "Well, those bus kids are dirty and rowdy," or "That guy has an earring and tattoos." We are to be servants to all people and to esteem *everyone* better than ourselves, the Bible says in Philippians 2:3. Ephesians 6:6 says, *"Not with eyeservice, as menpleasers; but as the servants of Christ, doing the will of God from the heart."*

Isn't that what Jesus did for us? When Jesus was here, He said, *"I seek not mine own will, but the will of the Father which hath sent me"* (John 5:30). What did Jesus do? The Bible says it was Jesus *"Who gave himself for our sins, that he might deliver us from this present evil world, according to the will of God and our Father"* (Galatians 1:4). Jesus died for our sins to fulfill the Father's will for our redemption. He did so willingly, lovingly. And each one of us can be forgiven of our sins because Jesus laid down His life for us. If He could do that for every vile human being that walked this earth, can't we humble ourselves to serve our fellow man?

It's just reasonable to serve Him when we think about what He has done for us.

Obeying God Is Always Best

"And the word of the Lord *came unto Jonah the second time, saying, Arise, go unto Nineveh, that great city, and preach unto it the preaching that I bid thee"* (Jonah 3:1–2).

God gives Jonah a second chance here. A few years ago my daughter-in-law wrote an absolutely beautiful song entitled "The God of Second Chances." The God of second chances—what a wonderful thought. He *is* the God of second chances. Here in our Bibles is living proof: Jonah got a second chance to get back into the will of God.

What do you think he did this time? Verse 3 records, *"So Jonah arose, and went unto Nineveh, according to the word of the* Lord*."* You see, God's will is found for us in God's Word. When God tells us He wants something done in our lives, it's simply a matter of saying, "Yes, Sir," to God. It's so wonderful to know that Jonah, who had missed the will of God in his life, now had a second chance. If you're out of the will of God, come on back. He will give you another chance too. If you have been going your own way, repent, acknowledge that God must have first place in your life, and surrender to do His will. Obey what you know His Word says to do, and He will guide you in the areas that do not seem so clear. Obeying God is always the best way to live.

6

When You Feel Personal Rejection

Personal rejection—it seems to hover like a dark cloud. Whenever a little sunshine promises to brighten and cheer, that cloud seems to drift in again, threatening rain. It's hard to shake its gloominess, because the cloud of personal rejection usually forms in stormy relationships, and relationship problems cause the deepest wounds and heartaches, particularly when family members are the ones who have abandoned or spurned you. Let's discover what God's Word can teach us about these times.

GENESIS 37:1–4

And Jacob dwelt in the land wherein his father was a stranger, in the land of Canaan. These are the generations of Jacob. Joseph, being seventeen years old, was feeding the flock with his brethren; and the lad was with the sons of Bilhah, and with the sons of Zilpah, his father's wives: and Joseph brought unto his father their evil report. Now Israel loved Joseph more than all his children, because he was the son of his old age: and he made him a coat of many colours. And when his brethren saw that their father loved him more than all his brethren, they hated him, and could not speak peaceably unto him.

Joseph was part of what we might call a dysfunctional family, and though a dark cloud always followed Joseph wherever he went, he seemed completely unaffected. It never rained on Joseph's parade. Joseph faced rejection over and over without sinking into gloom and despair. He always seemed to rise above it.

Since all of us have faced and will face rejection, we need to learn how to rise above it as well. After we look at some real-life scenarios of rejection, we will examine Joseph's life to see how he handled similar rejection.

Notice in Genesis 37:3 that it says, *"Now Israel loved Joseph more than all his children, because he was the son of his old age."* (Israel is simply another name God gave to Jacob. Whenever I mention Israel in this chapter, I am referring to the man not the country.) The Bible tells us that this man Israel loved Joseph more than all his other kids. He showed this extra affection for Joseph by making him a coat of many colors. When his brothers saw that their father loved Joseph more, they hated him and could not speak peaceably to him. So here is Joseph suffering rejection from his own brothers—the first of many recorded incidents of rejection in his life.

Rejection can come from many different sources. You may relate to one, many, or all of the sources we will detail on the pages of this chapter. It may cause pain just to read the scenarios, but we must honestly face the rejection we have experienced and learn how to deal with it successfully, as Joseph did.

LIVING ALONE, TOGETHER

Certainly one of the most tragic family rifts is a man or a woman rejecting his or her spouse for another to whom "love" is transferred. This other relationship may last only a short time—but one extramarital date is enough to sever the trust so vital to any marriage. Sometimes the unfaithful spouse chooses to walk out to be with the third person. Of course, that action is wretched and ungodly. I've seen, all too often, the horrible grief it causes the injured spouse and innocent children, but this is not the only kind of rejection that destroys marital relationships.

Each spouse comes to the marriage with a set of personal shortcomings, frailties, and idiosyncrasies to struggle through. If a couple never learns to manage their differences and harmonize their lives into one, they will grow further apart over the years rather than closer, as they should. Many married people live with one another for years in the same house but without a loving relationship. Perhaps they have grown tired of trying to work out their differences, or perhaps they just don't like each other. Something—or perhaps anything and everything—about the other spouse has become a turn-off. They live under the same roof, but they don't have a real home. It's merely a house that two people occupy. Though a third party may never have been involved in the estrangement, it is heartbreaking nonetheless, and the rejection felt by both spouses can be acute.

IN A FAMILY BUT NOT A PART OF THE FAMILY

It's tough growing up in today's world. Society seems to be creating a bigger gap between children and their family members, particularly as technology drives a plethora of distractions into the wedge growing between them. Rather than nurturing loving relationships, family members are disengaging to the point that young people feel isolated, misunderstood, and unloved.

Without the loving connection necessary to healthy relationships, children view their parents' unsolicited advice as intrusive, and tensions arise over the normal problems of everyday life—housekeeping, schoolwork, finances, etc. Add to those irritants personality differences, disrespect, favoritism, peer rejection, and sometimes even demonic influences, and you end up with some deep-seated conflicts that are difficult to resolve. Sometimes to avoid yelling and arguing, parents fail to address these conflicts, and children sink deeper and deeper into despondency or rage, depending on their inclinations. With their distorted perception they think, "I have insurmountable problems, and my own parents couldn't care less." Maybe you have been there yourself.

Some years ago we were all shocked to hear about the teenager that walked into a prayer meeting in Paducah, Kentucky, took out his rifle, and started shooting. Three girls were killed and five others were seriously injured; one is permanently paralyzed from the waist down. What goes wrong in the mind of a fourteen-year-old that makes firing randomly into a group of teenagers seem like the right thing to do? I'm sure it was not any *one* factor that caused this crime, but according to the investigating sheriff, the boy had always felt rejection. He had never felt wanted; he had never been part of the group or the "in" crowd. This is not the only incident of violent crime committed by young people in which statements were made regarding feelings of rejection.

When we hear of such things, we always ask "why?" Is the possible answer that the person was burdened by feelings of rejection? It's very likely. Among the common characteristics shared by all children who commit violent crimes is a strong feeling of rejection—rejection that generally begins in the home. Nothing could justify such acts of violence, but it is certainly true that rejection has a powerful effect on the human psyche.

FRIENDLESSNESS

Some of the closest ties we feel are those of friendship. We find camaraderie, acceptance, encouragement, and companionship in this delightful relationship. It is a wonderful gift of God to have a friend with whom you share similar interests and activities, one you entrust with your feelings, ideas, and dreams. That's why, when there is a breach in a friendship, we hurt intensely and long for restoration.

A number of years ago, I experienced such a breach of friendship. This person, someone whom I looked up to and held in very high regard, someone whose friendship meant a great deal to me, absolutely turned on me. I had done something this friend didn't like, and as a result, he just wrote me off. I received a letter that simply said, almost verbatim, "You're no friend of mine."

That hurt. It was like a knife thrust into my heart. I couldn't believe that in response to his misunderstanding of the truth, he would simply dispose of someone he had called "friend." It was just mind-boggling to me.

Having received such a slap, I sat there stunned, trying to think through my options. I could get angry, which in all honesty was the response I tended toward first. I could get bitter, allowing the thing to eat at me as I replayed it over and over. Or, I could do what I did. I simply wrote back and said, "I'm sorry to hear that I am no longer your friend, but I want you to know that you are still mine." By the way, the misunderstanding has long since been cleared up, and we are friends again, but I will never forget what that kind of rejection felt like—no more calls, no more encouraging conversations, no more sweet fellowship. It's painful and lonely.

PASSED OVER IN THE WORKPLACE

The workplace can be a place where you feel rejection—maybe on a regular basis. We've all heard of people caving in under the pressure and "going postal." "It's a dog-eat-dog world" may be an expression you can relate to regarding your work. Perhaps you didn't get the job promotion you believed you were the most qualified for. It is always true that when people compete for a promotion, someone gets the promotion and someone does not. Someone becomes the manager and someone does not. This may be of little solace to you, though, if you have been disappointed. Of course, you feel badly when you don't get selected for a job. The reasons don't matter: "You're not qualified," "You're overqualified." You know what it means. You missed it.

Now, think about your options here. You can take your loss as a personal rejection with an attitude that says, "They don't give me the respect I deserve. I should have been given the job." Or, you can take it as an opportunity to learn with an outlook that says, "It wasn't God's timing. He must have some more shaping to do in my life."

Let me warn you, though, if you decide to take it as a personal rejection, be very careful. Holding on to feelings of rejection is likely to cause bitterness to take root in your heart. You can play it over and over: "I shouldn't have been rejected for that promotion." "I deserved it." "I've been here longer." Each time the root goes deeper, but it doesn't change your job situation. The only thing that changes is your heart—and, believe me, it is not for the better.

We could go on and on with painful scenarios—not making a ball team, a singing group, or a cheerleading squad. We've all faced them, but one of the keys to life is how we respond to rejection.

Rejection Substitutes

There are many ways people handle rejection. Some of the behaviors listed below are common but very harmful. You might recognize yourself as you read through them. If you are displaying some of these responses to rejection, realize that they are only poor substitutes for the biblical way to handle the feelings you are experiencing.

LASHING OUT

Saul was the first king of Israel. When he began his reign, he was humble, an attribute upon which God based His selection when choosing a king for Israel. Later, he got puffed up and apparently thought he was above obeying the Lord.

God had instructed Saul to utterly destroy the Amalekites—no one was to be saved, and they were not to take a bit of spoil—but Saul disobeyed and saved the king and the best of the sheep and oxen.

As a result of his rebellion, God directed the prophet Samuel to bring Saul the bad news, "*For rebellion is as the sin of witchcraft, and stubbornness is as iniquity and idolatry. Because thou hast rejected the word of the Lord, he hath also rejected thee from being king*" (1 Samuel 15:23). "You're no longer qualified to be the king," God said.

I don't think we can imagine how rejected Saul felt at that moment, but his response was certainly not a godly one. Saul lashed out at Samuel. "They're taking my kingdom from me," Saul thought. He was so eaten up with rage and jealousy that he actually tried on several occasions to kill his successor, David, in an attempt to hold on to the kingdom he felt slipping from his grasp. Saul became bitter and delusional, hunting David like an animal, and finally died a broken man.

Lashing out at others is a typical way for some to handle their rejection, but as we can see from Saul's pitiful end, it leads only to more trouble.

EATING YOUR WAY OUT

Rejection causes such a horrible feeling of emptiness. Trauma comes—"I wasn't accepted," "It didn't work out," "I lost my friend," "I lost my job," "I didn't get my promotion"—and people try all kinds of things to fill the empty ache in their hungry hearts. One of these things is food. They try to eat themselves out of their troubles and worries, either binging or filling up on comfort foods like sweets. Of course, that doesn't work to ease the pain, and the repercussions of such splurges are obvious—or will be eventually.

ABANDONING YOUR MARRIAGE

Some people, when they feel rejected by their spouse, look for a new love to replace their spouse's love. Again, they are left with a big hole in their hearts that they try desperately to fill. They long to feel attractive and desirable, and when an opportunity arises to fill their yearning for love, they justify their actions. "All right, you may not love me, but I've found someone who does. I'm still attractive. I'll show you!"

By the way, there's nothing a spouse can do that gives you the right to give your love to someone else. It is just wrong. If your marriage isn't working out as it should, your response must be to seek out and follow wise biblical counsel to get it working right.

You may say, "Well, my spouse was unfaithful to me, so I'm going to be unfaithful just to get even." That's not how you respond to your spouse's unfaithfulness. You deal with it biblically. If you follow what God has set out in the Bible, your marriage can be saved as the problems are worked out. Things *can* change.

The beauty of ordering your life and marriage in accordance with the Scriptures is that as you work at it, you see things changing in your life. It can happen, but you can't just do what seems right to you. Rather, you must come to God and say, "Lord, my spouse and I need You. Help us work it out."

WITHDRAWING

In response to rejection, particularly relational rejection, some people go into hibernation. They retreat from the world thinking, "What's the use? Why try?" Or perhaps their reaction is to say, "I can't handle it. I'm just going to withdraw because the world is so harsh and cruel." But withdrawing only compounds the feelings of loneliness and rejection.

SPENDING MONEY

Ding! Oh the lovely sound the register makes as the drawer opens and the cashier hands you your change. You walk away with your bag of merchandise, and you feel so good—for a little while. But spending is just another temporary fix people try in order to quiet their rejected hearts. The end result is usually a heap of credit card debt and a bunch of stuff that didn't satisfy.

Perhaps you are thinking, "So that's my spouse's problem. Feelings of rejection!" That's not always true. Unbridled, reckless spending may simply be a lack of self-control, but often it is a response to feelings of personal rejection. "I'll do something that will give me pleasure," they think, even though the pleasure wears off long before the credit card bills arrive.

We could add any number of behaviors here that people resort to when they feel rejected, but none of them solves anything. They do nothing to bring the healing necessary. Let's turn our attention now to some helpful principles. What are the correct responses to rejection?

Rejection Solutions

The question is, "When I feel rejection, how should I handle it?" "My spouse doesn't want me, and my kids don't appreciate me." "My parents don't love me." "All my friends just seem to fall away." "I don't know if it is worth going on." Our minds can literally become overwhelmed with these negative thoughts and the feelings they engender. Thankfully, God has answers.

This is where we can learn from Joseph's life and his responses to rejection. In his example we see how God is able to work in our lives, even in difficult circumstances.

GO FORWARD

Jacob wept as he recognized the bloodstained coat—the beautiful coat he had made with his own hands for his special son Joseph. "Father, here is the coat we found. Do you know if it is Joseph's coat?" Jacob's sons left him believing that Joseph must have been torn up by a wild beast, when in reality, those jealous men had cast him into a pit and plotted to sell their little brother to the Ishmaelites. Since this is about a ten-chapter story in the Bible, I'll just give a quick synopsis.

When Reuben returned to the pit to find that Midianite merchantmen had already absconded with the young man, the men went back to their father with their fabricated story, satisfied that they were finally rid of their annoying brother.

If anyone had an absolute right to feel rejected, it was Joseph. He could have cried, "No one cares about me. My own brothers despise me. My daddy's not coming after me. What am I going to do?"

Then things went from bad to worse. The Midianites sold Joseph in Egypt at the slave market. Now Joseph really had a reason to cry, "Now, I'm just a slave. Why even go on?"

That's the attitude that many people take when things don't go their way: Why even try? But there's a reason for your hardships, so get a grip on yourself. Life's not over just because you have suffered a little rejection. You can go on, and that's exactly what Joseph did and why the Bible described him as a "goodly person."

Potiphar, the man who bought Joseph, was in charge of the king's guards. In Joseph, Potiphar saw a goodly person, not someone throwing a pity party, not someone whining, not someone griping. He saw a young man who said, "My brothers sold me, my daddy doesn't even know I'm alive, but I'm going to give life my best shot. I'm going to do my utmost to make my life really count for God right where I am." And that's exactly what he did. Genesis 39:6 describes the level of trust that Potiphar had in Joseph: *"And he* [Potiphar] *left all that he had in Joseph's hand; and he knew not ought he had, save the bread which he did eat. And Joseph was a goodly person, and well favoured."* Joseph worked himself up the line into the number one position in Potiphar's house.

A few years after I started the church, I wondered why some of the visitors from the previous week did not come back. Then it occurred to me, since preaching is the most public thing I do, these visitors probably didn't come back because they didn't like what I preached, the way I preached, or both.

Even though I'm a preacher of the Gospel, I'm capable of getting an attitude, just like anybody else. But, praise God, I've learned that even though not everybody is going to accept me, I don't have to give up on life, I can keep on going.

I say to everyone who is dealing with personal rejection, resolve to go forward regardless of your situation. Life may not be everything you want it to be. You may be suffering, but go on. Go forward. Make your life count. Do what you ought to do without regard for what has happened in the past—and do it with a cheerful attitude! That is the way Joseph did it.

To understand the context of the following solutions, you need to know a little more of Joseph's story. Joseph worked hard as Potiphar's slave in Egypt, yet he was falsely accused by Potiphar's wife and thrown in jail. Once again, Joseph was rejected!

While he was in jail, he interpreted a dream for two of Pharaoh's servants. When one of them was restored to his position in Pharaoh's house, Joseph pleaded with him to remember him to Pharaoh, but the servant forgot all about Joseph. Rejected again! For two years, Joseph remained in prison completely forgotten—until one night Pharaoh had a troubling dream.

Everyone was in an uproar! Not one of Pharaoh's counselors could explain the meaning of this dream, and heads were going to roll! Finally, Pharaoh's butler remembered the young man who had interpreted his dream in prison, and before Joseph knew what was happening he was standing before Pharaoh explaining the dream: The next seven years would be a time of plenty. The following seven years would be a time of famine. Joseph suggested that Pharaoh appoint a man to lay up food against the hard times ahead. Pharaoh put Joseph in charge. No one but Pharaoh himself was superior to Joseph at this point.

Joseph planned well, and during the famine, everyone came to Egypt to buy food from Joseph, among them were Joseph's brothers who had no idea what had become of Joseph.

Picture these men bowing before the second most powerful man in Egypt—in the world—asking for food. He spoke to them in Aramaic through an interpreter. So they had not the slightest clue that this man was Joseph, their brother, but he immediately recognized them. What did

Joseph do when he was faced with the men responsible for the tribulation he had suffered?

HE DID GOOD

"And Joseph said unto his brethren, Come near to me, I pray you. And they came near. And he said, I am Joseph your brother, whom ye sold into Egypt. Now therefore be not grieved, nor angry with yourselves, that ye sold me hither: for God did send me before you to preserve life" (Genesis 45:4–5).

Here was Joseph, holding in his hand the power of life or death over his brothers—the brothers who had hated him, who had plotted against him, who had turned his life upside down. Now the tables were turned. He was able to grant their request for food—or not—at his own whim. He had a choice to make.

Joseph asked his brothers to come near, and in their own language he said, "I'm your brother, Joseph." Can you imagine the shock they felt, standing there, their jaws hanging, as they tried to process what they had just heard? When it finally sank in that this was their brother, I'm sure they thought, "Oh, no! Joseph? Dare we even hope that he spares our lives?" They had no idea what Joseph might do to them.

Joseph simply said, "Don't worry yourselves. I'll give you the food you need." How about you, reader? Is that what you would have said?

Joseph's response to personal rejection was to do good to those that rejected him. This is hardly the first response that naturally comes to mind in the face of personal rejection. It is perhaps not the first response, but it is the proper one. It is the response of one who walks with God, who trusts Him with every aspect of his life. This is the response of someone who realizes that God has a purpose in every heartache and works all things together for good.

Do good to those people that reject you. If your boss rejects you, your best response is to do good to him. You don't have to agree with everything the boss does or with every decision he makes. No one ever does. But you shouldn't respond by fighting or scheming revenge. You don't have to hurt anyone. Just work harder. When it is in God's timing, things will work out for you. In fact, there is more hope for your future when you respond properly. A godly response leaves a lasting impression in the minds of your boss and your coworkers.

When your spouse does you wrong or rejects you, you don't have to fight fire with fire. Nothing is ever resolved that way. Two fires just make things hotter! Model yourself after Joseph. Do good to your spouse. Jesus gives us this instruction: "*Do good to them that hate you, and pray for them which despitefully use you, and persecute you…* [and also to those that] *say all manner of evil against you falsely for my sake,*" in Matthew 5:44 and 11. Hold no bitterness—no anger whatsoever—against those that reject you, because if you do, you'll never get ahead. Learn instead to do good to them.

HE SAW GOD IN HIS CIRCUMSTANCES

Another way to avoid feelings of personal rejection is to see God at work in your circumstances. We learn this from Joseph, as well. In Genesis 45:6–8, Joseph said, "*For these two years hath the famine been in the land: and yet there are five years, in the which there shall neither be earing nor harvest. And God sent me before you to preserve you a posterity in the earth, and to save your lives by a great deliverance. So now it was not you that sent me hither, but God: and he hath made me a father to Pharaoh, and lord of all his house, and a ruler throughout all the land of Egypt.*"

He said, "My brothers, don't worry about it. I know that my life is in God's hands and that God was working this whole situation to bring about good. He has made me second in command here in Egypt so that I could provide for you, my dad, and all my siblings. This was not your doing. It was God's."

During all those years of hardship, Joseph knew that God had a plan in all of it. You see, when Joseph was a very young man, God gave him some dreams. Joseph knew, without a doubt, that those dreams were from God, and through it all, he continued to believe in his dreams. When he was sold as a slave, he knew God wasn't finished with him. When he was thrown into prison, he knew that it was part of God's plan for his life. When it seemed that everyone had forgotten him, he knew that God hadn't. He held on to those dreams all those years knowing that God would bring them to pass. He never wavered in his faith. He knew God had it all under control.

That's the way to look at life. God is in control of my circumstances and yours. We don't have to manipulate our circumstances, nor do we have to despair that God has forgotten us. We can believe with absolute assurance that God is going to work out everything as He intends.

He knows where you are, He knows the rejection you have faced, and He is working it all for good—if you love Him. Yes, people have let you down, but God hasn't. Just continue to love Him. Keep looking up.

HE MENDED BROKEN FENCES

Be quick to mend your fences. Take heed, my friend; a hole in your fence will allow all kinds of unwelcome varmints into your pasture to cause you trouble. You've got to mend those fences!

Joseph got right to the task of fence mending when he was reunited with his brothers. "*And he* [Joseph] *fell upon his brother Benjamin's neck, and wept; and Benjamin wept upon his neck. Moreover he kissed all his brethren, and wept upon them: and after that his brethren talked with him*" (Genesis 45:14–15). You can see by all the neck hugging going on here what I mean by fence mending. Joseph forgave those rascals who had done him wrong!

I'll warn you though, fence mending is hard work. You're going to need some help. You see, rejection carries an intense sting. It makes us feel inferior and inadequate. It cuts right to the heart because it calls into question our own sense of self-worth. For these reasons, fence mending does not come easily for us. That's why you're going to need some help.

You'll need the Holy Spirit to give you the tools necessary to mend those broken-down fences. You're going to need love, joy, peace, longsuffering, gentleness, goodness, faith, meekness, and temperance. Does this list sound familiar? That's right, you need the fruit of the Spirit when you have broken-down fences. You need the Holy Spirit's filling to produce the "tools" you'll need for such a tough job. Beg Him to help you do what you can't do in your own flesh. By all means, friend, if only for your own sake, mend those fences.

HE FOCUSED ON GOD

I have one last rejection solution to offer. This response is really the base that undergirds all the others: stay focused on God. In Genesis 50:20–21, Joseph provides a synopsis of the whole situation: "*But as for you, ye thought evil against me; but God meant it unto good, to bring to pass, as it is this day, to save much people alive. Now therefore fear ye not: I will nourish you, and your little ones. And he comforted them, and spake kindly unto them.*" Joseph said, "Look, brothers, you meant it for evil, but God meant it for good." The devil fires his darts at us intending to do us evil, but God takes those very "darts" and uses them to produce something good in our lives. Remember this familiar verse? "*And we know that all things work together for good to them that love God, to them who are the called according to his purpose*" (Romans 8:28).

God works all things together for good, but what is the "good" He is trying to accomplish? You can find the answer in the next verse: "*For whom he did foreknow, he also did predestinate to be conformed to the image of his Son, that he might be the firstborn among many brethren*" (Romans 8:29). He is using "all things"—even the bad things—to make us more like Jesus, to make us more lovely and usable. He has only your best in mind.

If you have been saved and born into God's family, absolutely nothing can happen in your life that God does not allow. Be encouraged that He can take the fragments of a broken life and create something beautiful—if you'll let Him.

Conclusion

Rejection is a horrible thing. We all want to be loved and appreciated, and it hurts when we feel unworthy of esteem or affection.

Take heart. There is Someone who understands exactly how you feel. Jesus left the glories of Heaven to come to this earth so that He could die to redeem sinful mankind, but the people that should have been most prepared to receive Him, those that should have been eagerly awaiting Him did not recognize Him as the perfect, sinless Son of God. John 1:10–11 tells us, *"He was in the world, and the world was made by him, and the world knew him not. He came unto his own, and his own received him not."* Worse yet, the ones for whom He came to die despised Him and rejected Him. Isaiah 53:3: *"He is despised and rejected of men; a man of sorrows, and acquainted with grief: and we hid as it were our faces from him; he was despised, and we esteemed him not."*

You may feel like no one cares for or loves you or that no one is interested in your life. Jesus cares. He will receive you if you will have faith to believe that He is the Christ, the Son of God and accept Him as your Saviour. He will forgive your sins so that you can know you are accepted into the beloved family of God. When you have the acceptance of the Lord, you quickly find out that you don't depend on the acceptance of any man or woman like you used to. God makes the difference in our lives.

7

When You Feel Conflict in the Home

LUKE 15:11–16

And he said, A certain man had two sons. And the younger of them said to his father, Father, give me the portion of goods that falleth to me. And he divided unto them his living. And not so many days after the younger son gathered all together, and took his journey into a far country, and there wasted his substance with riotous living. And when he had spent all, there arose a mighty famine in that land, and he began to be in want. And he went and joined himself to a citizen of that country; and he sent him into his fields to feed swine. And he would fain have filled his belly with the husks that the swine did eat: and no man gave unto him.

This chapter deals specifically with the parent/child relationship. It is very common for children to feel that their parents don't understand them, and for a good reason: parents oftentimes feel as though they *don't* understand their children. They wonder how these people who have grown up in their home could think so differently than they think.

Although their memories may be fading, they do remember the difficulty they sometimes had in trying to communicate their feelings to their own parents. But now, as parents, they sometimes wonder, "What's wrong with this present evil generation?" It's as though they are looking at some new breed of human being. They cannot understand why their son wants to wear spray-painted jeans and their daughter wants to wear black nail polish.

Parents aren't the only ones mystified. Young people feel absolutely convinced that their parents came to America on Noah's ark. They probably had Moses and Elijah as playmates when they were kids. What else could explain the antiquated ideas these parents have regarding life?

The tumultuous 1960s gave birth to a name for this phenomenon. They called this difference in viewpoints between young people and their parents "the generation gap," and although today's young people may be less demonstrative in their defiance than the hippies of the sixties, studies show the gap is widening, particularly as it pertains to moral values. It goes much deeper than tight pants and black nail polish.

Though some of the issues dividing parents and children now have shifted with the culture, the age-old problem is the same. Jesus spoke of it in His story of the prodigal son in Luke 15:11–16, "*And he said, A certain man had two sons. And the younger of them said to his father, Father, give me the portion of goods that falleth to me. And he divided unto them his living. And not so many days after the younger son gathered all together, and took his journey into a far country, and there wasted his substance with riotous living. And when he had spent all, there arose a mighty famine in that land, and he began to be in want. And he went and joined himself to a citizen of that country; and he sent him into his fields to feed swine. And he would fain have filled his belly with the husks that the swine did eat: and no man gave unto him.*"

A Communication Gap

Notice something about the communication between this prodigal son and his father. "*And the younger of them said to his father, Father, give me the portion of goods that falleth to me.*" In other words, he said, "Hey, Dad, I want what's coming to me now. I've had enough of this waiting around for you to pass away. I'm going to get the inheritance sooner or later anyhow. I'm a man. I'm ready to get out on my own."

Look at this text and see the request for what it really was. This son wasn't *asking* his father for the inheritance; he was *demanding* it. He wanted his portion of his father's goods, and he wanted it now! To me, the obvious conclusion is that there is a communication problem here. They might have talked, but they just couldn't understand each other.

Communication problems, however, are not confined to children. In fact, parents bear most of the burden when it comes to family communication.

Five Communication Barriers

1. Children feel their parents do not value them. Kids may feel that they're an imposition or that they're unwanted. "My parents don't need me and don't want me. I am just a bother to them."

There are many reasons children feel this way, and they are usually due to the manner in which parents relate to their children. Parents sometimes brush their children off when they need to talk. To parents, the child's questions and problems may seem annoying and trivial. To the child, they are monumental, and when they are dismissed as unimportant, the child may feel that he is the one who is insignificant and small.

He also feels demeaned when parents address sensitive issues in front of other people, even if they are family members. This communication mistake causes the child to lose trust in his parents, the people whom he should trust most. Of course, a lack of trust will hinder further communication with the injured child.

Sometimes parents act resentful or irritated when they have to take time to deal with the child's needs. Things like helping with math problems turn into a nightmare, and the child feels flawed and inferior simply because he needs help. As he grows older, his problems grow too. Bigger issues mean that he is going to need help with understanding life and making good choices, but he will be hesitant to come to his parents for any kind of help if he feels that he is nothing but a bother to them.

Probably the main communication deficiency that causes children to feel devalued is the way parents handle their anger. Children do act in ways that can cause us to become angry, but blowing up does not make any headway in sorting out problems. In fact, hollering is a very ineffective way to communicate because children learn over time how to tune out their parents' angry outbursts. That's not to say that these tantrums do not cause harm—they certainly do. Yelling or name-calling causes emotional wounds that become calloused over the course of years, hardening the child's heart to any attempts the parents make at communication.

Think of the hundreds of times that exchanges like these might have occurred by the time a child becomes a young adult, each one confirming in his mind his own worthlessness. As the child gets older, he becomes resentful of these parents who made him feel inferior. He perceives them as insensitive and apathetic, and as you can imagine, this emotional wedge between the parent and child severs any real communication regarding the important issues of life.

2. Children are often expected to fit into the parents' mold. Many times, parents, because of their own frustrating childhood, seek to live vicariously through their children. They missed opportunities to play the instrument or to be on the basketball or volleyball team or the cheerleading squad. They wanted to be a doctor, nurse, preacher, missionary, or something else, but things didn't turn out the way they dreamed. So, they are determined to make their children into what they wanted to be.

Children who live with this kind of pressure may feel that their parents don't understand them or appreciate their individual gifts, abilities, dreams, and desires. They may feel that they have to rebel to be seen and heard. Obviously, resentment or withdrawal could result, neither of which is conducive to good communication.

Parents, don't force your kids into a mold you designed. Rather, put them in God's hands and let Him mold their lives. I'm not at all suggesting that you don't give direction and guidance to your kids. Parents are to be the primary molding influence on their children's character and love for God, but they are not to determine their gifts and calling. That is God's job to do.

3. Parents don't have time to give to their children—or perhaps I should say they don't give the time they have to their children. You might wonder, "That rebellious son of mine, where did he get his thinking process? He's like a stranger to me." Maybe you don't understand him because he *is* a stranger to you. You never took the time to get to know him. Now, he's a teenager, and you want to help him make good decisions, but there is no talking to him. Why should he feel comfortable talking to someone who does not know him, someone who has neglected him for years?

What is more important than spending time with your children? Entertainment? A career? This may come as a surprise to you, Mom and Dad, but making money is not more important than making memories with your kids! I would not take a million or even ten million dollars for the relationship that I have with my son.

May I offer a little insight to those of you who still have children or teens at home? When your children become adults, that's when you begin to think about what your children's lives could have been like, should have been like, and you realize it's too late. If you begin, at that point, trying to communicate with them, you've waited too long. You'd better make sure that you do your homework while the kids are still at home, or you will be a remorseful parent when you reach my stage in life.

There's no excuse for not spending time with your children *now.* Dad, this is particularly true for you. In Ephesians 6:4, the Bible gives the responsibility of training the children to fathers. Dad, you need to tell yourself, "Raising these children is primarily my responsibility, not my wife's."

To those of you who do not yet have children: if you don't have time to invest daily in their lives, don't have kids. Don't cheat the children you bring into this world out of a dad or mom because your interests and activities are so important to you that you can't do a proper job of parenting.

4. The world's indoctrination builds barriers between parents and their children. We live in the age of information, and children, now more than ever, are inundated with information—all kinds of it. They have seen it all on television and the Internet. They become steeped in their subculture as they submerge themselves in Facebook and YouTube. They are worldly-wise and self-sufficient, smugly echoing the culture's attitude, "My mom and dad just don't understand. They're just not as smart as I am. After all, Mom needs help just to turn on the computer." You need only to read the back of a cereal box to see that kids are bombarded with the attitude "You're in charge." "Why talk to parents when we know it all?" seems to be their mantra.

5. Deficient relationships break communication. Parents do a lot of talking. They tell their kids to do their homework, clean their rooms, and take out the trash. They tell them they left the lid off the toothpaste, forgot to turn off their bedroom light, and wasted the milk they left on the counter. They say the same things over and over again. They talk plenty! The problem is, with all their instructing, informing and nagging, they sometimes forget to ask questions: "What do you think about that?" "Why do you seem frustrated by this?" "How did you feel when she treated you that way?" They forget to find out about these unique individuals God has placed in their homes. Listening is a good start.

Parents, you can't wait until your kids are teens to begin the process of developing a good relationship with them. It won't happen. We send our kids to school when they are five years old, and within just a few years, the relationships they develop with their peers become their most important ones, particularly if they do not have strong relationships at home. When they want to find out the truth about sex, relationships, jobs, money, and even Christianity—if they care to understand it at all—they will go to the people they trust, the people with whom they have strong relationships—their friends—because they don't feel comfortable talking to their parents.

Tragic Consequences

I've already mentioned that this breakdown in communication causes resentment, withdrawal, disdain, or rebellion in kids because they feel that their parents don't understand them, and maybe don't care to understand them. In extreme cases, they feel that their parents are oppressive people who live just to make their lives miserable. These kids react to their resentment by turning their backs on their parents and everything they stand for. When they do, they are more likely to turn their backs on other authorities as well. There is a great chance that they will end up living lives that are immoral and unrighteous, thus scarring themselves for life.

Kids who are less prone to outright rebellion might simply feel detached from their parents. So they float downstream with the crowd, looking for fulfillment, trying to please their peers because no one at home took the time to connect with them. As they drift, they may eventually end up in the same place as the blatantly rebellious child—in sin and ruin.

In either case, there is missed potential because the child is not living out God's plan for his life. There are no winners when children are left alone to do their own thing because parents want to be left alone to do theirs.

All of it causes heartbreak. "...*A wise son maketh a glad father, but a foolish son is the heaviness of his mother*" (Proverbs 10:1). When the prodigal went his own way, he caused his father heartbreak, and in the end, his own heart was broken as well. Really, he had never been happy to begin with. He was always discontented and selfish, searching for satisfaction.

How sad this story is! Think about all of the benefits that this son had. He had everything he could have ever wanted. He was comfortable and protected in his father's home, but he wanted to push out of the protection that he viewed as restraints. "Eat, drink, and be merry, for tomorrow we die" was his philosophy. He wanted to be something that he was not yet—his own man (funded with Dad's money, of course).

The moment that we value *things* more than people, or *pleasure* more than responsibility, we are headed for trouble and turmoil. It doesn't matter what your age. When you take control of your life and make up your mind that you want to live it up for a while, when you put your personal desires, your pleasures, and your interests above the values of the Bible, you're headed down a slippery slope that will bring you to nothing but heartache.

THE GRASS IS ALWAYS GREENER SOMEPLACE ELSE

More than likely, the kid thought his dad had unfair expectations—always requiring him to work and carry his own weight, or maybe the son thought that the father was too strict, intruding on his territory, and denying him his rights. Whatever his problem, the prodigal was one who always seemed to have his face pressed up against the glass, feeling that he was missing something and longing to go out and get it. He couldn't wait to be free.

I guess all of us have experienced some of these frustrations on our journey to adulthood, some to a greater degree and some to a lesser. All of us at some time or another have thought that our parents just didn't understand. I remember going through that in my own teen life.

I'M OLD ENOUGH

Back in the ancient days when I was a kid, you could get a driver's license at age 15, at which point I began working my parents. "Dad and Mom, I'm 15 now. I need a car."

My parents would say, "This is crazy! You don't need a car."

Undaunted, I kept up this harassment for quite a while. "Hey, Mom and Dad, you don't understand! I *need* a car." Ticking the items off on my fingers, I would reiterate the reasons I desperately needed a car. "Number one, I won't be loitering around on the streets. Number two, it'll help me get to school and work faster than walking or taking a bus or thumbing a ride. And number three," I explained, "if you give me a car, then, in my friends' eyes, you will be perceived as the most loving, caring parents ever."

Finally, the day came when my worn-down father said, "You've been asking for a car, and I've decided to give you one." My mind conjured up images of a shiny, new BMW! I really wasn't sure what it was going to be, and I didn't care. I was thrilled! I was going to have my own car!

While I was imagining cruising up to my friends in a hot convertible, my dad had an entirely different idea. He owned a gas station in northeast Washington D.C., and every now and then, somebody, unable to pay a repair bill of $50 or $100, would just abandon their car. Yeah, you guessed it. That's how he got my car. It was a Henry J—a 1951 Kaiser Henry J—lime green, no less. You should have seen my face!

You can't even imagine how ugly this car was. I had a hard time believing it myself. When my buddies and I would go anywhere, we parked it a couple of blocks away from our destination and walked the rest of the way. It was humiliating.

What my parents did to me was nothing short of child abuse. There was definitely a breakdown in communication somewhere in that process! I'm kidding, of course, but the point is we all go through conflict. We all battle with feelings of discontentment and selfishness, but oftentimes in those turbulent teen years, the rift in our family relationships widens into a huge gap. For it to go on widening would probably mean that some of the serious consequences we discussed are just down the road. Something must be done to mend the breach. Good intentions will not get the job done. You need to begin taking steps *today* to improve your communication and restore your relationships.

Developing Good Relationships in the Family

As you have probably noticed, communication is the key to having a good parent/child relationship; therefore, establishing good communication early in the child's life is of utmost importance. This doesn't necessarily happen instinctively, unless you had a good model in your own family. For most of us, it takes a conscious effort to learn communication skills and apply them to everyday situations. It takes time, but do it for your children.

HANDLING PROBLEMS

Many times communication breaks down when problems arise, and of course, they will arise—usually on a daily basis. Learn how to handle problems with a biblical approach. Yelling or screaming is not the way to go about it. As I mentioned earlier, this approach breaks down communication and causes emotional wounds. It is also sinful. In Colossians 3:21, the Bible says, "*Fathers, provoke not your children to anger, lest they be discouraged.*"

Keep sinful anger out of your home. You say, "That's easy for you to say, you don't have the brats I have in my house. My kids just won't obey. They just make me so angry sometimes." If you ever yell at your son or daughter, your anger is out of hand. You say, "You don't know my kids! The only way you can handle them is to yell, and sometimes you have to actually shake them."

That's not true. There's a better way to handle problems with kids. You teach them respect for your God-given authority, rather than condition them to disobey. Yes, that's what yelling and screaming does—it conditions them to respond wrongly.

This is a typical scenario: Dad tells Johnny to take out the trash, only to come back later to find that the trash is still sitting where it was before. This time Dad yells, "Johnny, take out the trash!" But Johnny is busy playing. He doesn't care about taking out the trash—that is, until Dad gets really angry and yells, *"Johnny, take out the trash right now, or you're in big trouble!"* Johnny will take out the trash then. But what Dad has done is condition Johnny to ignore him until his blood pressure is up and his face turns red.

To avoid this type of conditioning, you establish rules (discipline) and consequences (punishment). Established rules in your home help you avoid anger. If you say, "Take out the trash," and your child doesn't do it the first time, he has breached the discipline you established. Therefore, you must carry through with the consequence (punishment). There is no yelling, no screaming, just the natural consequence of his transgression. It may be that Johnny now has to take out the trash in every room and wash every garbage can inside and out. He may think his options through more clearly if an hour of his playtime is spent washing garbage cans.

I never yelled at my son. I don't mean he didn't do some things that irritated the daylights out of me, but I never got angry with him because there was no need for it.

Consider another scenario: your son comes strutting into the house with blue hair and oversized pants that he's not big enough to fill, trying to act like the man that he isn't. He's responding to peer pressure and feels that he has to look this way because everyone else does. In the boy's mind, he has to wear baggy pants, a black jacket, and chains like all of his buddies, because he wants to do his "own thing." (Ever notice that a teen's expression of "individuality" is looking just like all the other "individuals" in a particular crowd?)

When Dad sees his son he yells, "Look here, kid, you aren't going to have blue hair in my house!"

The immediate and sharp response is, "Why not?"

"Because I'm the dad. You're coming with me! We're going to get your hair dyed back to its natural color."

Now, tell me something. Do you think that after the dad dealt with the situation this way, the family lived happily ever after? Sure, the dad dealt with the problem. He may have proved that he is bigger, stronger, and more powerful because his son had to give in, but did he communicate effectively with his son?

He stopped his kid from looking weird, but that didn't change a thing about the way the boy felt about himself. It certainly didn't improve the parent-child relationship, and we all know it. As presented, this is a hopeless situation, and sadly, it's all too common.

I'm not saying that the dad shouldn't have done what he did, but dyeing his hair and buying him new jeans didn't have an impact on his heart. The key is to reverse the process. When you concentrate on dealing with the inside, the externals will fall into place as well. It might be better to start here: "Son, sit down. We need to have a talk." When you communicate, you both have plenty of opportunity to clarify whatever the other doesn't understand.

LISTENING

The first step to talking out problems is to listen, "...*for out of the abundance of the heart the mouth speaketh*" (Matthew 12:34). If you're going to deal with problems, you have to know what is going on inside your child, and the only way to find out is to listen. Good communication always begins with listening. In the previous scenario, the dad might have started with a few questions: "Why do you think we set down guidelines in our home for appearance?" "What are your reasons for wanting to dress this way?" "Can we come up with a solution here?" Then, depending on what he finds out, he has a reference point for the discussion, rather than demands. Parents, when you treat your child with respect, he will be more ready to hear what you have to tell him from the Bible, and you will have taught him an invaluable lesson on communication.

Being a good listener is important to both sides of any discussion. If you are under the authority of your parents, you should listen to them. Parents establish rules and guidelines for your protection and to keep the home running smoothly with everyone doing his part. You may be surprised at the wisdom your parents have gleaned from their many years of experience. They were teenagers once, and they made some mistakes too. They would rather you learn from their mistakes than to make your own and live with the consequences. Give your parents the benefit of the doubt. They love you.

GIVING RESPECT

Parents, learn to treat your child with respect. When you have to handle problems, focus on your child's many positive qualities, rather than on how angry you feel. It is so easy as a parent to focus only on the negatives when you deal with character flaws and wrongdoing. Therefore, it will take a conscious effort to bring something positive into the conversation, maybe some affirming words: "I appreciate what you're saying." "I can see that you have given this some thought." Treat your child with dignity, the way you would want your boss to treat you if you needed a reprimand at work.

Children, you must respect your parents even when you believe they do not understand. The Bible says, "*Children, obey your parents in the Lord: for this is right*" (Ephesians 6:1). You say, "Well, that's fine, but my parents aren't always right." That may be true, but here is God's rule: parents don't have to be right to be obeyed. It's just that simple. You obey your parents, regardless of whether you have differing opinions, just because they're your parents.

God gets the highest place of honor and respect in your life, but your parents should have second place, even if you feel they don't deserve it. God put them in that position, not you. But, rest assured, He will bless you if you choose to do what is right.

I'll never forget a lesson my son taught me years ago. He was dating a girl in college and I was trying to find out what she was like. I fired questions at him: "What is she like?" "Does she have blond hair?" "Blue eyes?" "What does she look like?

His first response was, "Dad, she loves her parents." That was the primary thing that he was looking for in a friend, that she would love her parents. He knew that if she respected her parents, she probably would not have a hard time with his position of biblical authority as a husband. Love your parents. It's a good quality for all young people to have. Don't allow yourself to be angry or bitter toward Mom or Dad, just love them enough to give them the respect that God intended.

MAKING TIME FOR EACH OTHER

Make time for your family. As kids grow older and become more independent, it becomes more difficult to make time for each other, but there's no substitute for *time.* For either the parents or the kids to say, "Well, I'm just busy all week long, but I'll try to cram it in on Saturday night," just won't work. Think about what you can do to develop a relationship with your child.

What fun things can you do together? What serious things can you do together? A really great family activity, one that promotes communication and understanding and, at the same time, touches hearts is Bible study. The critical thing is time together. You ought to be willing to make it the highlight of the schedule, not the chore that must be squeezed in between "more important" events.

EXERCISING PATIENCE, HUMILITY, AND LOVE

I think this is a great definition of parental love: "patiently enduring through the childhood so that you have a good friend when they, too, are adults." Parents, remember your children are not adults yet. So be careful about setting your expectations too high. Have a plan for the quality people that you want your children to become, and spend a lot of time with them, lovingly nurturing those qualities in their lives. As they mature, you can raise your expectations. If they fall short, calmly help them back up and point them in the right direction again.

If there's a communication breakdown in the home, rather than blame the kids, I suggest that you humbly look inside and ask yourself, "Am I doing something that is causing my children to feel detached?" When a child says, "Mom and Dad don't understand," it indicates frustration and disengagement. You have a broken relationship—if there was one to begin with. Take time with each other and expend the energy necessary to work it out. I promise you it's worth it.

For a young person hoping to find a way to improve his relationship with his parents, my best advice would be to give the parents another chance. Give them honor and respect. The prodigal son learned this lesson, but he had to learn it the hard way.

Let's pick up the story of the prodigal son at verse 17, *"And when he came to himself, he said, How many hired servants of my father's have bread enough and to spare, and I perish with hunger!"* Things hadn't worked out as well as the prodigal had imagined. Now a defeated young man, he decides with a broken spirit and contrite heart that it's time to return home.

Notice what the son said when he came to himself. *"I will arise and go to my father, and will say unto him, Father, I have sinned against heaven, and before thee, And am no more worthy to be called thy son: make me as one of thy hired servants"* (Luke 15:18–19). He determined to talk humbly and respectfully to his father—quite a contrast from the beginning of the story where he demanded his inheritance right then and there. His hardships opened his eyes to how blessed he had been. It's too bad it took the hogpen to wake him up. Young people, don't wait until you are wallowing in the "hogpen" to make things right with your parents. Do it now.

We learn a lot from the reaction of the father in this story. In Luke 15:20–24, Jesus said, "*And he* [the prodigal son] *arose, and came to his father. But when he was yet a great way off, his father saw him, and had compassion, and ran, and fell on his neck, and kissed him. And the son said unto him, Father, I have sinned against heaven, and in thy sight, and am no more worthy to be called thy son. But the father said to his servants, Bring forth the best robe, and put it on him; and put a ring on his hand, and shoes on his feet: And bring hither the fatted calf, and kill it; and let us eat, and be merry: For this my son was dead, and is alive again; he was lost, and is found....*"

When the son humbled himself and asked forgiveness, the relationship was immediately restored. That's love.

To both parents and kids I say, swallow your pride and ask the other for forgiveness. Let the other person know that you want to understand and you want to be understood. Demonstrate that you are willing to work out a solution and that you are confident that, together, you can deal with any problem.

You can have wonderful family relationships if you will practice patience, humility, and love, but the Spirit of God must produce those qualities in your life as you yield to His control. Are you daily seeking to be filled with the Spirit?

In the next chapter, we will discuss walking in the Spirit to defeat sinful passions. The same principles apply to defeating the pride and selfishness that hinders relationships. Read it and determine to begin living that way today.

A NEW BEGINNING

The Bible describes the best relationship that a person can have with God as a parent/child relationship. Each of us is, by birth, like the prodigal son in the parable. We have wandered far from God, and we must come to ourselves like the prodigal son and seek forgiveness from our Heavenly Father. The wonderful thing is that, when you do humble yourself and come to Christ for forgiveness, God is ready and willing to forgive. The Bible says, "*Ye are my witnesses, saith the LORD, and my servant whom I have chosen: that ye may know and believe me, and understand that I am he; before me there was no God formed, neither shall there be after me. I, even I, am the LORD; and beside me there is no saviour*" (Isaiah 43:10–11).

Ask God for help every day as you work on communicating with your family and building a relationship that, when childhood has passed, will be an enduring friendship.

8

When You Feel Lust Consuming Your Life

1 PETER 2:9–12

But ye are a chosen generation, a royal priesthood, an holy nation, a peculiar people; that ye should shew forth the praises of him who hath called you out of darkness into his marvellous light: Which in time past were not a people, but are now the people of God: which had not obtained mercy, but now have obtained mercy. Dearly beloved, I beseech you as strangers and pilgrims, abstain from fleshly lusts, which war against the soul; Having your conversation honest among the Gentiles: that, whereas they speak against you as evildoers, they may by your good works, which they shall behold, glorify God in the day of visitation.

As you can tell from the title, this chapter deals with a subject that crosses the breadth of all of humanity—lust. There's not a human being alive who hasn't experienced the temptation to dwell on lustful thoughts or dabble in the sin to which these thoughts lead.

LUST IS NOT NECESSARILY EVIL

Lust, which simply means "strong desire," can be experienced for any number of things—either bad or good. You can lust for material things. For instance, you may see someone else's brand new vehicle and think, "Wow, that's nice! If only I had one of those, I'd be so happy!" Or you can lust for immaterial things such as position and power. Some people waste their lives trying to achieve, striving to get to the top. And worse, these people often lose their families in the process, just so they can feel a sense of pride and accomplishment. Nothing you or I could attain would be worth that.

I couldn't list all the objects of people's lust—a big bank account, higher intellect, university degrees, retirement, good health. The objects of desire are not wrong in and of themselves, but your motives in wanting them may be. Ask yourself, "Why do I want those things, for the glory of God, or for my own glorification?"

Obviously one of the things we can lust for is sexual gratification. When we use the word *lust* in today's vernacular, it generally carries the connotation of a desire for evil things, particularly illicit sex, and in this chapter, I deal specifically with that meaning of the word *lust*.

I don't mind telling you that I sat at my computer for three hours just trying to figure out how in the world to begin discussing lust. I finally decided that the best starting point is a discussion of God's standard for moral living. God makes it clear that believers are to be different. He calls us to a higher standard of living: *"Be ye holy; for I am holy"* (1 Peter 1:16).

A Call to Holiness

Peter begins verse 9 of our text with the word *"But,"* which signifies the contrast that is to follow between the unsaved, about whom he had spoken in the previous verses, and saved—Christian—people whom he now addresses. He writes, *"But, ye* [Christians] *are a chosen generation, a royal priesthood, an holy nation, a peculiar people, that ye should shew forth the praises of him who hath called you out of darkness into his marvellous light.*" He gives the force of application to these words in verse 12: "*Having your conversation* [manner of life] *honest among the Gentiles: that, whereas they speak against you as evildoers, they may by your good works, which they shall behold, glorify God in the day of visitation.*" He's saying that a person who gives testimony of personal salvation is to live differently from how the unsaved world lives. He is to walk to the beat of a different drum.

Abstain!

The Lord gives us a succinct directive 1 Peter 2:11: "*Dearly Beloved,* [a term used only for Christian people] *I beseech you as strangers and pilgrims, abstain from fleshly lusts, which war against the soul.*" Abstain? Why? Isn't sexual desire a natural phenomenon that happens to all of us? Isn't it a need, almost as much as the food that we eat and the air we breathe?

The Battlefield Has Been Set Up, the Lines Are Drawn

Notice the last phrase of 1 Peter 2:11. It tells us that these desires "*war against the soul.*" That is why we are to abstain from them. The body's desires are not wrong or sinful in themselves, but those desires can become perverted, tempting even Christians to satisfy them in ways that are absolutely contrary to the Word of God. It becomes a battle—for your soul, for your very life—against your own flesh. The devil, because he desires to destroy you, uses your fleshly desire for sex as one of his most effective tactics.

I mentioned in a previous chapter that the devil has set up a world system to influence our thinking. He has provided allures that ignite sexual urges and that pervert them. Everywhere you look—billboards, television, newspapers, magazines—you find the advertisement industry exploiting America's lust for sex to tout their products. The entertainment industry seems to be wholly given over to perverting society as they sink to new depths everyday. Even the news media feels the need to present more shocking images and stories to boost ratings. Do not be ignorant of Satan's devices. The warning is to all of us: the devil is after you, and if you think you are exempt, you have already placed yourself in a vulnerable position.

Why do we have this war of the flesh? In Ephesians 2:1–3, the apostle Paul wrote, "*And you hath he quickened* [or made alive], *who were dead in trespasses and sins; Wherein in time past ye walked according to the course of this world, according to the prince of the power of the air, the spirit that now worketh in the children of disobedience: Among whom also we all had our conversation in times past in the lusts of our flesh, fulfilling the desires of the flesh and of the mind; and were by nature the children of wrath, even as others.*" According to this text, the reason we are prone to lust is that it is our nature to do so. We are born with a sinful nature. Sin is not something you have to teach a child. It's part of who he is.

Those who have accepted Christ have become partakers of a new nature, a Christ-like nature, but those who have not accepted Christ do not have this resource to combat sin. They try in their flesh, but the old nature is weak and often fails.

If you can't honestly say that you have accepted Christ as your own personal Saviour, then, as a friend, I urge you to do so today. It is through Him alone that we can have victory over the sinful desires of our flesh.

Becoming a Christian is no guarantee that you will not run up against the sinful temptations that are common to everyone. But a personal relationship with Christ does mean that, as a believer, you have the ability, through Him, to overcome any and every temptation that knocks at your door. Christians do have power available to them to abstain from fleshly lusts.

The Battle Is Ours to Fight

Unfortunately, many Christians succumb to sin because they do not stop the downward spiral that begins when lust takes hold in their hearts and minds. Study this progression: "*But every man is tempted, when he is drawn away of his own lust, and enticed. Then when lust hath conceived, it bringeth forth sin: and sin, when it is finished, bringeth forth death*" (James 1:14–15).

David was a man after God's own heart, but he let down his guard—maybe because he thought he was exempt from doing wickedness. When lust took hold on his heart, it was not long before he was drawn away of his own wicked desires. You can see the downward spiral played out before your eyes in David 's life.

It was the time when kings went to war, but King David was not where he should have been. Instead we find him strolling out onto his rooftop overlooking the city to enjoy the cool of the evening. He wasn't doing anything wrong, he just wasn't doing what he was supposed to be doing.

David stretched his weary body and took in the sunset. As he observed the sights and sounds of the city, his eyes stopped at the home of one of his valiant soldiers, Uriah. There he saw Uriah's wife, Bathsheba, bathing on the deck of their porch. Rather than turn away, he lingered there watching her, and it caused him to lust. He couldn't get this woman out of his mind. She was so beautiful. He dwelt on what it would be like to have a physical relationship with her, to the point of obsession. Finally, he decided to act on his lust.

He sent his messengers to go get her. They said, "But she's a married woman."

"I just want to talk to her, " David said, and he ordered his servants to obey.

Bathsheba came to the palace of the king unsuspecting. David forced himself upon her and committed adultery. His adultery led to the murder of Uriah and the death of the illegitimate baby—a very heartbreaking story indeed!

Lest you think that lust is confined to men, consider the story of Potiphar's wife who lusted after Joseph. In Genesis 39:7–9, the Bible says: *"And it came to pass after these things, that his master's wife cast her eyes upon Joseph; and she said, Lie with me. But he refused, and said unto his master's wife, Behold, my master wotteth not what is with me in the house, and he hath committed all that he hath to my hand; There is none greater in this house than I; neither hath he kept back any thing from me but thee, because thou art his wife: how then can I do this great wickedness, and sin against God?"*

LUST LINGERS

Potiphar's wife *"cast her eyes upon Joseph."* Notice that lust usually starts with the eyes, which is why pornography is a multi-billion-dollar business in America today. Americans cannot get enough X-rated movies, Internet sites, and magazines. The effect these explicit materials have on men and their marriages is devastating.

Pornography degrades women, reducing them to sexual objects rather than elevating them to the queenly position they ought to have in every home. Men, if you indulge in this trash, you will consider your wife deficient compared to the women you are watching: perfect creatures masquerading for the camera. Your wife will never live up to the fantasies that you dwell on. Mark it down, if you are filling up on this garbage, your marriage is headed for the rocks. "But I'm not about to divorce my wife," you say. I don't think any man starts out planning for divorce. But that's exactly where lust leads, because thoughts about the "other woman" linger, haunting the obsessed man, until he does the unthinkable.

Seeking fulfillment by giving place to these sexual lusts actually results in unfulfilled desires. The relationship that should be satisfying the desire for sex becomes inadequate in comparison to the fantasies of the one straying. When marital intimacy wanes—and it will when a man allows his mind to create a fantasy world—the discontented spouse will go looking for intimacy somewhere else. What was meant to fill a desire actually created one—one that cannot be fulfilled no matter how many illicit relationships a person has.

As people are living for the fulfillment of their own selfish pleasures, they are actually becoming enslaved to a self-imposed bondage. Christian people are finding themselves in addictions programs trying to break free of the habit that has become a cruel oppressor. Do you remember this verse? *"For he that soweth to his flesh shall of the flesh reap corruption"* (Galatians 6:8). You will reap what you sow. It's just not worth the cost.

LUST IS SELFISH

Be careful about your love life. What do you love? God is sickened when we allow our affections to stray to the wickedness this world has to offer. *"Love not the world, neither the things that are in the world. If any man love the world, the love of the Father is not in him. For all that is in the world, the lust of the flesh, and the lust of the eyes, and the pride of life, is not of the Father, but is of the world. And the world passeth away, and the lust thereof: but he that doeth the will of God abideth for ever"* (1 John 2:15–17). Dwelling on lust leads to self-absorption and self-gratification, which is very, very dangerous. It led David to adultery. If you are living a life consumed with lust, there is no way possible that God could be pleased with it.

Tips on Winning the Battle

How do we get victory over these powerful desires when it is our nature to lust? The big difference in the lives of Christians, as opposed to the lives of unbelievers, is not that we don't have lusts, but that we don't fulfill the lust when it arises. We are able to stop it immediately when it comes because of the help Christ offers us. I'll give you five things that you can do to gain victory over destructive, life-consuming lust.

1. Assume full responsibility for your life. I've heard from a number of people who have gone to a psychiatrist or psychologist for help that the first thing they do is drag you back into your childhood to explain away and excuse the problems you are having now. Unfortunately, it is true for many people that they have had some horrific things happen to them, and I'm not minimizing them one bit. But I am saying, "Okay, so what can you to do about it now? You can't keep living in the past. You can't keep using it as a crutch or as an excuse to avoid facing today." Don't shift the blame for your problems to your childhood (or any other event in the past), no matter how horrible it might have been. If you know that your present condition is not good, then change. It's time to let go of the past and take responsibility for your life today.

You can't shift the blame to your spouse either. Stop making excuses. "My wife is as cold as a fish, that's why I'm looking for love." Forget the excuses, it's your problem. Until you're willing to accept full responsibility for the lust consuming your heart, you'll be haunted by it for the rest of your life. You'll be giving in to it constantly.

God says to abstain from lusts. Do you understand what He means? He is not saying abstain from sexual fornication; He is saying abstain from the very desires that lead to those acts. If you have accepted Jesus Christ as your Saviour then you're a part of a holy people, a royal priesthood. Christians are held to a higher standard. A Christian is not even to think on adultery, much less commit it.

Change, and start living the reality of who you are in Christ. God can work to change you—if you will let Him. The first step is to take responsibility for your thought life.

2. Stop feeding your lust. The Bible says, "*But put ye on the Lord Jesus Christ, and make not provision for the flesh, to fulfil the lusts thereof*" (Romans 13:14). Don't make provisions for lust. As someone once observed, you can't stop a bird from flying over your head, but you can stop her from building a nest in your hair. You may not stop every fleeting lustful thought, but you don't have to linger over the thought, encouraging its germination and nurturing its growth.

There are a number of things that you can do to help decrease the number and frequency of lustful thoughts. The first thing is to destroy all magazines and videos that feed your appetite for unholy things. Burn them; don't give them away to someone else, to ruin their life. Destroy them. Today, just viewing cable television is enough to incite powerful desires. Monitor everything that goes into your mind. It is your responsibility. No one can do it for you.

The second thing is to be careful about where you go. If you go to those wicked, ungodly bars and strip joints, quit doing it, abstain from it. If you drive by those places on the way home and are tempted, start taking a different route. Don't walk past the magazine rack if you find temptation there. Avoid all temptation.

The third thing you have to do immediately is cut off any potential relationship with any person of the opposite sex outside your own marriage. Do not allow yourself to be placed into a compromising position with someone of the opposite sex. If you're starting to feel emotionally involved with someone who is not your spouse, you can be 100 percent certain that is heading down the wrong path. Stop it. Don't wean away from it. Just cut it off. Abstain from it, completely and immediately. The Bible says, "*That ye put off concerning the former conversation the old man, which is corrupt according to the deceitful lusts*" (Ephesians 4:22).

3. Beware of the danger in the workplace. On this same point, be careful at work. Never share home or family problems with anyone in your office. There are problems that arise in any marriage. We've all experienced them. But instead of looking outside the home for sympathy or companionship, the responsible act is that you and your spouse work it out together or seek counsel if you can't resolve the problems yourselves. Dozens of times I've seen the destruction of people's lives when they do not follow what I am advising now. Don't ignore this biblical counsel. The cost is too high.

4. Never dine out alone with the opposite sex. You say, "Wait a minute, what about secretary's day?" My advice is that you take out twenty secretaries, but don't take only one. Gather the largest crowd you can, and treat them all. Or, if there's only one secretary in the office, call your wife to join you.

"Well, in my job I have to dine alone with persons of the opposite sex." Change jobs.

"Well, don't get so fanatical. Everybody does it." It's almost never true that "everybody" does anything, and even if it were true, you should be the exception. I've never in my life, outside of courtship, taken someone of the opposite sex to dinner, and I don't ever plan to. Make it a rule.

Of course the same principle is true for a lady. You don't have any business going to dinner with a man who is not your husband. Don't accept a ride from a man if you'll be in the car with him by yourself, even if you're broken down on the side of the road! Let him fix your flat tire, or ask him to get help for you, but don't accept a ride. You don't even want the appearance that something is going on. Be careful.

If you're single, go on double dates only. There's safety in numbers. You say, "That's okay for kids who are 13 or 14, but I'm older. I'm 19 or 23 years old, and I don't need that." You need it even more. You might say, "What's wrong, don't you trust me?" I don't trust the flesh—yours or mine. Unfortunately, when we get saved we still have our old sin nature, and we take it on every date we have. Don't give lusts an opportunity to take hold of you.

5. Be careful to guard your eye gate. The Bible says, "*whosoever looketh on a woman to lust after her hath committed adultery with her already in his heart*" (Matthew 5:28). The Bible also says, "*Lust not after her beauty in thine heart; neither let her take thee with her eyelids*" (Proverbs 6:25). Sure, he may be handsome, and she may be beautiful, but that doesn't mean you have to indulge. Be extremely careful about the things you watch. I hear about parental guides for monitoring and controlling children's television viewing. The truth is that parents need monitoring and controlling as much as the kids do—maybe more! There's no difference between my lustful desires and a teenager's lustful desires, except mine have had more experience. So don't think that it's okay to watch something that you would not allow your children to see, and don't try to convince your kids it's okay either.

If you have cable TV, HBO, and that other rotten stuff with X-rated films coming into your home, cancel it. I hear people say, "But I don't look at that stuff. It was just part of the package." All it takes is a fleeting moment as you are changing channels, and that image is in your mind for a lifetime. If you're being honest, why have it if you're not going to watch it. Get rid of it. It can destroy your family.

Be careful when you are traveling too. It happens all the time: people go to motels and watch trash that they wouldn't watch at home, just because it's available and they're alone. I read an article talking about a religious convention that was held in a particular town. One hotel that hosted the people attending the convention sold more X-rated videos through the cable TV than during most other conventions they had accommodated. Abstain from it. Don't make provision for it. Say as the psalmist said in Psalm 101:3, "*I will set no wicked thing before mine eyes.*"

6. Run! The Bible says in 2 Timothy 2:22, "*Flee also youthful lusts.*" I mean run! Get out of there!

I didn't finish the story about Joseph that I referenced earlier in this chapter. When Joseph refused Potiphar's wife, he turned to leave but she grabbed onto his coat. Joseph let her have it and ran out of the place. Do as Joseph did. Even if you have to leave something behind, leave. The Bible commentator, Matthew Henry, said, "It's a whole lot better to lose your coat than your conscience."

The Bible instructs us to crucify our affections. "*And they that are Christ's have crucified the flesh with the affections and lusts*" (Galatians 5:24). If something catches your eye, and you find yourself thinking inappropriately, instantly crucify yourself. Picture yourself on the cross, dead. A dead man cannot dwell on those thoughts. Stop wrong thoughts dead in their tracks, and turn your attention to God—quote a verse; sing a song; do whatever you must.

If you are spiritually weak, you will not have the strength to run. How are you going to find strength like the strength Joseph displayed? The answer is found in Galatians 5:16 (a verse you ought to underline and put a star by; I've done both): "*This I say then, Walk in the Spirit, and ye shall not fulfil the lust of the flesh.*"

7. Walk in the Spirit. What does it mean to walk in the Spirit? It simply means that you are living a life that is led by the Spirit. The Holy Spirit will never lead you to do something that is contrary to His Word.

I cannot stress enough how important it is to fill your life with the Word of God. "*Let the word of Christ dwell in you richly in all wisdom; teaching and admonishing one another in psalms and hymns and spiritual songs, singing with grace in your hearts to the Lord*" (Colossians 3:16). This verse is parallel to the passage in Ephesians that instructs us to be filled with the Spirit. "*And be not drunk with wine, wherein is excess; but be filled with the Spirit; Speaking to yourselves in psalms and hymns and spiritual songs, singing and making melody in your heart to the Lord*" (Ephesians 5:18–19).

We need the filling of the Spirit to give us power to conquer our fleshly desires. To be filled with the Spirit, you must fill your heart and mind with the Word of God—read it, memorize it, obey it—and daily beg God to fill you with His Spirit.

Another important step is yielding yourself to the Spirit. You are a slave to whoever controls you. For that reason, the Bible tells us that sin should not hold the position of master in your life. "*Let not sin therefore reign in your mortal body, that ye should obey it in the lusts thereof. Neither yield ye your members as instruments of unrighteousness unto sin: but yield yourselves unto God, as those that are alive from the dead, and your members as instruments of righteousness unto God. For sin shall not have dominion over you: for ye are not under the law, but under grace*" (Romans 6:12–14).

Yielding yourself to God requires dying to yourself. When your old nature rears its ugly head—die. Realize that your old sin nature was crucified on the cross and that you do not have to obey it any longer. When a lustful thought about another person comes, stop yourself and say, "I am no longer a slave to my sinful nature. I don't have to dwell on this." Resist the flesh. Then, think loving thoughts about your spouse and pray for her. Let your desire be only toward your spouse.

Instead of yielding yourself to your sinful desires, yield yourself to God. Make Him your Master. The Bible tells us in Romans 12:2 to yield our bodies as *"a living sacrifice."* Tell God, "Here I am, Lord. These are Your hands and Your feet, Your lips and Your eyes, Your heart and Your mind to control. Do with them as You will." You may have to remind yourself many times a day to die to your own desires and to yield yourself to God. It is not your human nature to do so, but a new nature lives within you if you are a Christian, and you can yield to the righteousness of Christ. *"And that ye put on the new man, which after God is created in righteousness and true holiness"* (Ephesians 4:24).

This is walking in the Spirit: filling your heart and mind with God's Word, dying to your own will and desires, praying for His strength, wisdom, and leading, and then choosing every step you take.

Each step should be a step in the Spirit, not a step in the flesh. That means if you have a choice between walking down the magazine aisle or walking past it, you choose to walk past it. That means if you have a choice between watching a program with a lewd scene or turning it off, you choose to turn it off. The man who daily lives his life this way will be strong enough to rise above temptation because He has equipped himself to do so. This life can be yours if you will pay the price to be in God's Word and in prayer and to humbly yield every step to Him.

If you fail, confess your wrong thoughts, desires, motives, or deeds to the Lord and get things right with Him. Sin that is not confessed and forsaken grieves the Holy Spirit—your source of power. Don't cut yourself off from your power source.

Christian living is a matter of your will, not your emotions, and not your feelings. It is submitting your will to Jesus Christ and His Word. You cannot do it on your own. Trying to overcome lust by yourself is an exercise in futility. Paul said, "*I can do all things…*" and some people stop there. "Through self-esteem, self-effort, self-righteousness, I can do it." But that's not where Paul ended. He said, "*I can do all things through Christ which strengtheneth me*" (Philippians 4:13). Knowing the Lord and yielding to Him makes all the difference in our lives.

Conclusion

The truth is that controlling the sin of lust is no different from controlling any other sin. If you try to do it in your own strength, through the determination of your own will, you will experience only temporary success at best—if you have success at all. But when you turn control of your life over to God, then the battle is no longer your will against your flesh, but it is the Holy Spirit of God against your flesh. "*For the flesh lusteth against the Spirit, and the Spirit against the flesh: and these are contrary the one to the other: so that ye cannot do the things that ye would*" (Galatians 5:17). The Holy Spirit's help is the only hope of lasting victory over lust, or any other sin. "*…we are more than conquerors through him that loved us*" (Romans 8:37).

9

When You Feel Guilt Ridden

In this chapter we are going to pick up where we left off with Joseph's story in chapter six. The brothers still do not know that the young ruler overseeing the food sales in Egypt is their brother Joseph. Imagine their confusion and grief when Joseph demands that the men bring Jacob's youngest son Benjamin back to Egypt.

GENESIS 42:18–23

And Joseph said unto them the third day, This do, and live; for I fear God: If ye be true men, let one of your brethren be bound in the house of your prison: go ye, carry corn for the famine of your houses: But bring your youngest brother unto me; so shall your words be verified, and ye shall not die. And they did so. And they said one to another, We are verily guilty concerning our brother, in that we saw the anguish of his soul, when he besought us, and we would not hear; therefore is this distress come upon us. And Reuben answered them, saying, Spake I not unto you, saying, Do not sin against the child; and ye would not hear? therefore, behold, also his blood is required.

And they knew not that Joseph understood them; for he spake unto them by an interpreter.

Chapter 6 dealt with the subject of rejection, particularly Joseph's rejection. You'll remember, his brothers rejected him because he was their father's favorite son and conspired to sell him into slavery to get rid of him. Now Joseph is in charge of the food supply these brothers need to keep their families alive, and they are at his mercy. In this chapter, we are going to look at this story from the brothers' perspective—the perspective of the guilty.

Lies and Deception

It's a horrible atrocity to seriously think about selling your brother. But let's be honest about it; how many of us, when we were growing up, thought about selling our younger brothers or sisters to anyone that would take them for five or ten bucks? You can probably identify with Joseph's brothers. The difference is that his brothers actually did it!

It seemed like a good idea at the time, but then they had to face their father. He would certainly notice that Joseph was missing from the dinner table. So, they killed an animal, took Joseph's special coat, and dipped it into the animal's blood. With the bloodstained coat in hand, they came back to their father. "We haven't seen Joseph, but we found this coat. Isn't this Joseph's coat?" Of course, Jacob, who had made the coat of many colors especially for his favored son, knew right away that it was his. Just as the brothers had planned, Jacob assumed that Joseph—the son that he loved so dearly—had been torn up by a wild beast. But it was all a lie.

Just one lie. That's all it was—just one lie to cover up their sin of selling their brother. But the brothers carried the guilt of that lie and their evil act for over twenty years. I'm reminded again of Galatians 6:7, "*...whatsoever a man soweth, that shall he also reap.*" We can't get away with anything with God. We may think we're getting away with something when we lie; we may think that it's no big deal, that no one saw us, but whatever "it" is, it's still there and it still troubles us—for years or even decades, as was the case with Joseph's brothers.

Do you remember their story? In the dream that Joseph interpreted for Pharaoh, God had revealed that Egypt and the surrounding lands would go through seven years of famine. Pharaoh put Joseph in charge of preparing for the hard times ahead, and having planned well, Joseph was now in charge of selling the food stockpiled in the government storehouses. When Jacob heard of the plenty in Egypt, he instructed his ten eldest sons to go down to Egypt and buy food before the family starved to death.

Twenty-some years had passed since these men had plotted to sell their brother, and they had no idea what had become of him. Everything was different about Joseph as they stood before him now. He was twenty years older, probably in his mid- to late thirties, and powerful—second only to Pharaoh. They had no idea that this young ruler to whom they spoke through an interpreter was their brother.

Joseph, who recognized his brothers immediately, demanded details about their family. His heart melted when they mentioned his little brother Benjamin. He longed to see him. So, he told them they must bring back their youngest brother to prove that they were not spies.

The men knew this request would be a great burden on their elderly father, who had already lost one of his beloved Rachel's sons. How could they ask him to send Benjamin whom he had protected so carefully all these years? But they could see no alternative. They needed food desperately, and they had nowhere else to turn.

This is where our text begins with the brothers feeling the weight of the onerous assignment before them. The idea of talking their father into parting with Benjamin brought back the horrible images of what they had done years before. They remembered Joseph's terror as they overpowered him, stripped him of his coat, and threw him into a pit that was too deep and too slippery for him to climb out of. But it was his bitter cries that haunted them. The screams of their desperate brother crying to them from the pit had rung in their ears for nearly a quarter of a century.

Now we find them feeling guilty and remorseful. "His blood is required at our hand," they said. "All this hardship that has come upon us is because of what we did. Why did we ever do such an evil thing? Why?"

Two Great Hounds

Notice their confession in the text. They said, "We are truly guilty," and immediately memories of the terrible crime they had committed against their own flesh and blood flooded back. John Phillips said of guilt and memory, "These are God's two great hounds to bark at the door of the soul." When we do something wrong, right away, guilt sets in. Even if the guilt of that moment fades over time, when tribulation comes, the memory sifts through its files and pulls up our evil deeds to remind us of wrongs that still need to be made right. Our conscience says, "Look what you've done. This distress is the punishment you get." That is what happened to Joseph's brothers. They had always carried a nagging fear that they would be found out, and to them this seemed to be the day of reckoning. Their guilt was still rebuking them after all those years.

Guilt is a relentless nag. The head of a mental institution in London said, "I could release half of my patients if I could but find a way to get rid of their sense of guilt, because guilt is so overwhelming and has a lot of consequences that come with it."

You may feel guilty about something in your past right now, or perhaps something in your present. What do you do? Can you rid yourself of guilt, or must you carry a sense of guilt for the rest of your life?

Understanding Guilt

The theological definition of guilt, according to Strong's book on systematic theology is, "to be deserving of punishment or obligation to render satisfaction to God's justice for self-determined violation of the law." When I violate God's laws, I *am* guilty.

With this fact of guilt comes the feeling that I deserve punishment and the fear that I will get what I deserve. Therefore, guilt can also be defined as feelings of sinfulness, evil, wrongdoing, or failure to measure up to certain standards. We've all experienced feelings of guilt. It's the electricity that pulsates through your body when you look at something you weren't supposed to see, the memory that nudges you as soon as you close your eyes to go to sleep, the black cloud that hovers over your head no matter how sunny the day. When I feel guilt, it is because I know I've done wrong—whether the wrongdoing is real or imagined.

Why Do I Feel So Guilty?

Guilt sometimes results from committing an offense contrary to your own standards—standards which may or may not come from the Bible. These may be rules that we have set down for ourselves or that others have set down for us. You might have come from a family where you attended church every Sunday, no matter how sick you were. You lay in the pew with your feverish head in your mother's lap, but you were there. Now, you lie in a hospital bed after surgery and feel guilty because you are not in church. Cognitively, you realize that your absence is unavoidable, but emotionally, you feel that you are doing something wrong because you have been conditioned to feel guilty in this situation.

Feelings of guilt might arise because of failure to meet expectations. Some parents might say, "We worked with you on your school work, we've been praying for you, and we expect you to get 100% on this test today." The child does his best but comes home with a 90% and feels like a failure. He feels guilty for failing to achieve the parents' expectations, and because it was a matter of prayer, the child feels as though he has disappointed God as well.

By the way, if you are a parent, you must be careful that you don't place unfair expectations on your children. You have to be careful about setting a standard for A's when your child is a B student. Of course, you must use discernment. I don't mean that you just look the other way when he brings home C's if he is capable of A's or B's, but be careful that you do not impose *your* will on your children and set them up for guilt and failure as they try to meet unrealistic expectations.

A Violated Conscience

Violating our conscience also causes feelings of guilt to arise. We find this principle in Romans 14:23, "*And he that doubteth is damned if he eat, because he eateth not of faith: for whatsoever is not of faith is sin.*" We can follow this principle for things that are not clearly spelled out in the Bible. When the Bible says plainly, "Thou shalt not," you just don't do it. It's clear from Scripture, and you know exactly what God expects from you. But there are some things in the Bible that are not so clearly defined. There are things that two people can disagree on and neither one be wrong.

In Romans 14, the specific issue is whether or not eating meat that had been offered to idols is a sin. Eating this meat offended some Christians because they felt that the idol worship with which the meat had been associated somehow tainted it. Others, because they understood that this worship was to a god that didn't exist, took the opinion that the meat itself was not sinful, and they had no problem eating it. Paul told them, "If your conscience bothers you, if you have doubt in your mind whether or not you should partake, don't eat it." The principle is that whatever you do, you do it by faith, otherwise you are violating your conscience and you are guilty of sin because you are going ahead with something that you feel is wrong to do.

My point is that it is possible for your conscience to bother you even though the thing you feel guilty about isn't necessarily wrong.

Good Guilt?

Some say, "Let your conscience be your guide." That is a principle for matters that are not mentioned in Scripture, but for those that are, let the Scriptures be your guide. You ask, "Aren't the Scriptures and your conscience the same?" No, your conscience ought to line up with what the Scriptures say, but for most people that is simply not the case because they don't even know what the Scriptures say.

Furthermore, your conscience can be seared so that sin doesn't bother you anymore. I'm sure you've experienced that. The first time you did something wrong, you felt very bad. The next time you did it, the feeling of guilt was much less intense. After awhile, you felt only a mild twinge or nothing at all.

The guilt we experience from the sources mentioned previously may or may not be legitimate, but the guilt we feel when we break Scriptural principles is. In fact, God initially gave His law so that we *would* experience guilt.

Some people think the law was given so that people can obey it to earn their way to Heaven. Not on your life—thank the Lord—because none of us has ever kept every point of the law. It would be impossible to get to Heaven if keeping the law were the means.

In Romans 3:19, the Bible says, "*Now we know that what things soever the law saith, it saith to them who are under the law: that every mouth may be stopped, and all the world may become guilty before God.*" The purpose of the law was to bring a sense of guilt in having violated it.

It was given that sin might feel exceedingly wrong when we commit it. Why would a loving God want us to feel that way? Guilt is such a horrible feeling. So is touching a hot iron with your hand. In fact, it is so painful that you immediately draw your hand back from the source of pain. That is God's intention in giving us a sense of guilt over our sin. When we feel such an unpleasant emotion, we are not as likely to repeat the act that caused it.

Actually, God has shown Himself to be loving and merciful in giving us the law—though there is no way possible we are able to keep it—because the guilt we feel over our failure leads us to the solution for the sin that damns our souls to Hell. "*Wherefore the law was our schoolmaster to bring us unto Christ, that we might be justified by faith*" (Galatians 3:24).

When we choose to live contrary to the Bible, we *are* guilty. It's that simple. And our sense of guilt is a God-given help in turning us to the Saviour. For those of us who are already saved, guilt is a deterrent from the sin that destroys our lives. Legitimate guilt—feelings of guilt that come from breaking God's laws—is a blessing and a help.

You Don't Have to Live in Guilt

Again Joseph's cry rang in the brothers' ears. This time they weren't remembering the boy in the pit; they were frozen in stunned silence as they watched tears stream down their brother's face. "It is I, Joseph, your brother whom you sold." The brothers trembled, for their greatest fear had come to pass. Here before them stood the young man who had haunted them for so long. They knew that this time Joseph was in control. They could not overpower him as they had before. They were at his mercy. To their amazement, that is exactly what the brothers found—mercy.

Joseph came near to them and assured them he was not angry. All was forgiven. Their relationships were mended. In fact, Joseph brought every member of his family to Egypt to take care of them. For seventeen years they enjoyed the prosperity of Egypt together—until one day.

In Genesis, chapter 49, we read that Jacob died and left the twelve brothers alone, and that's when doubt began to resurface. "*And when Joseph's brethren saw that their father was dead, they said, Joseph will peradventure hate us, and will certainly requite us all the evil which we did unto him*" (Genesis 50:15). Because they knew that Joseph loved his dad, and his dad loved Joseph, the brothers figured Joseph would turn on them. "*And they sent a messenger unto Joseph, saying, Thy father did command before he died, saying, So shall ye say unto Joseph, Forgive, I pray thee now, the trespass of thy brethren, and their sin; for they did unto thee evil: and now, we pray thee, forgive the trespass of the servants of the God of thy father. And Joseph wept when they spake unto him. And his brethren also went and fell down before his face; and they said, Behold, we be thy servants*" (Genesis 50:16–18). They were truly repentant of their sin and got the relationship right with Joseph. That one horrific act committed almost forty years earlier haunted the brothers all those years until it was made completely right.

A Solution That Works

You don't have to continue in guilt and torment.

"Do you mean to tell me that I can get rid of all my guilt? I can get rid of all of my deserved punishment?" Yes, that's exactly what I mean.

"Is it possible that I can walk around a free man?" Yes.

"Are you saying that with all of my sins, all of my problems, all the ungodly things I've done, I can still get rid of that guilt?" The answer, thank God, is yes.

Romans 8:1 says, "*There is therefore now no condemnation to them which are in Christ Jesus, who walk not after the flesh, but after the Spirit.*" When you get saved by putting your faith in Jesus Christ, God credits all of your sin to Jesus' account. He became the guilty One and died to pay the penalty for that guilt so that you could go free. He paid for all of it. You don't deserve His unearned favor, and neither do I, but Jesus died on your behalf because He loves you.

You may think, "I don't need it." Be careful. Someone has said that the greatest of sins is to be conscious of none. "*If we say that we have not sinned, we make him a liar, and his word is not in us*" (1 John 1:10). "Well," you say, "I've never done anything bad enough to deserve Hell." The Bible states otherwise: "*Wherefore, as by one man sin entered into the world, and death by sin; and so death passed upon all men, for that all have sinned*"

(Romans 5:12). The Bible says that we *all* deserve death because we are all guilty. The death it refers to here is not physical death, but spiritual, as described in Revelation: *"And death and hell were cast into the lake of fire. This is the second death. And whosoever was not found written in the book of life was cast into the lake of fire"* (Revelation 20:14–15).

Friend, if you have not already, follow the steps that God has provided to remove your guilt. Christian, the steps are the same for you. Find the forgiveness you need to free you from the oppression of guilt.

Three Step Cure for Guilt

1. **Admit your sin to yourself.** Often we see the by-product of our guilt and believe those things to be our problem. Distress is one of the by-products of guilt. God often brings pain into our lives to make us examine ourselves, as Jacob's brothers did. When hardship came into their lives, the first thing they remembered was their sin. Other by-products are anger and depression caused by the burden guilt heaps upon us. Blame shifting and lying go hand-in-hand with guilt as well. Have you said any of the following? "It's not my fault." "I didn't do it." "Someone else started it." "They made me." Blame shifting and lying are just other ways of saying, "I don't want to admit what I did."

Substance abuse often accompanies guilt as a means of drowning out guilt's unpleasant feelings. Relationship problems are also very common when one carries the guilt of hurting another. I could go on and on listing the problems that keep company with guilt, but the underlying problem is sin, and the first step in dealing with it is to acknowledge it as such. Quit making excuses. The clear principle in the Bible is that as long as you cover or justify your sin, you will have no forgiveness.

After King David sinned against God, he said this: *"For I acknowledge my transgressions: and my sin is ever before me. Against thee, thee only, have I sinned, and done this evil in thy sight"* (Psalm 51:3–4). When God sent the prophet Nathan to confront David with his sins of adultery and murder,

David had to stop lying to himself. With his ugly deeds exposed, he was forced to look at what he had done.

He did just that; he acknowledged that he had sinned, and then he went a step further: he admitted that his sin was wicked. You may be able to salve your conscience saying, "What I did wasn't that bad." God sees it differently. The Bible says in James 2:10, "*For whosoever shall keep the whole law, and yet offend in one point, he is guilty of all.*" You are every bit as guilty as David because you have broken God's law. You nailed Jesus to the cross with the sin that you are trying to justify. It's time to recognize your sin for what it is—a disgraceful transgression of God's law and an offense to God Himself.

2. Confess your sin to God. Sin that is not confessed drags guilt on further and further, causing many of the problems we just discussed. When we do not confess and forsake sin, we build a wall between God and ourselves, and eventually God simply allows the sinner to continue in wicked, ungodly things. In Romans 1:28 we read, "*God gave them over to a reprobate mind,* [a mind rejected by God] *to do those things which are not convenient* [not becoming]."

Confess your sin to God (confession means to agree with God). See your sin as God sees it—wicked and injurious. When you confess, you admit openly that you are guilty before Him. You admit that what you have done is sin and that you want to turn 180 degrees away from that sin.

For the believer, it is just a simple matter of asking God to forgive you of your sin and forsaking that sin. First John 1:9 says, "*If we confess our sins, he is faithful and just to forgive us our sins, and to cleanse us from all unrighteousness.*"

For the unbeliever, the next step after confessing that you have sinned is to confess Christ. The Bible says, "*That if thou shalt confess with thy mouth the Lord Jesus, and shalt believe in thine heart that God hath raised him from the dead, thou shalt be saved*" (Romans 10:9). Confessing the Lord Jesus means agreeing that Jesus is God, as the Bible says, and accepting Him as your own personal Saviour.

3. Seek reconciliation with others that you may have wronged. That may be a spouse, a child, a friend, a parent, a teacher, or an employer. The Bible says, *"And herein do I exercise myself, to have always a conscience void of offence toward God, and toward men"* (Acts 24:16).

It's one thing to ask God for forgiveness: "Oh, Lord, forgive me; I've done wrong. Forgive me for the way I acted at work, for the way I treated my wife. Forgive me for all of it, God." But it is another thing to get it completely right. You're not done when you seek God's forgiveness. If you have sinned against someone else, you must go to the injured party and confess the sin to him as well.

It's important. Guilt is as oppressive as anything known to man, and when it's allowed to remain, people get caught up in a vicious cycle, trying to rid themselves of it anyway they can—except the right way. That's why people so often get to a point where they think, "Okay, I'm guilty, I'm wrong," and they'll drink some more, lash out again, or make up more lies. These things, of course, only add to the weight of their guilt. If you are on that merry-go-round, you need to get off. If it is at all possible, you must go back and make things right.

During my turbulent teens and twenties, I did a number of wrong things. I wasn't saved, and I just didn't live the right kind of life. Thank the Lord, accepting Christ changed my life completely.

Many years later, I was preaching about guilt, and suddenly I flashed back to a little shopping center in Arlington, Virginia. I had gone into a store with some friends, and I walked out with something under my coat. The item was only worth a couple of dollars back then, though today it would be worth more, but it bothered me. I knew I was wrong. I knew I had cheated someone. In a private prayer, I said, "I'm saved now, God, but although I'm forgiven, I realize that I need to get things right with those whom I have offended."

Ten or fifteen years had passed since my crime. Regardless, I wrote a letter to the people who owned the store and said, "When I was a teen, I stole something out of your store. I know that was wrong. I have since become a Christian. God has forgiven me, but I would like to ask you to forgive me as well. I've enclosed a ten dollar check to cover the two dollar item that I stole." Here was a written confession! I was scared to death I would have the police knocking on my door. But I was able to make right a wrong and remove the guilt of that deed.

I've had this question posed to me: "I've had an affair. Should I ever tell my spouse?" The answer is yes, absolutely, beyond a shadow of a doubt, 100 percent of the time. I know that answer is contrary to what you are likely to hear from worldly counselors, but according to biblical principles, it is the right answer.

"Keep it to yourself," I heard from a radio counselor, "so that you don't burden your spouse with it." Wrong! The Bible says marriage makes two people one, and when one of the two involves a third party in the marriage, that spouse has broken the covenant promise made before God. Hiding that, pretending that it never happened, is living a lie, which is wrong for a few reasons.

First, it is a lie. How can God bless that? Second, trust can never be re-established in a relationship built on lies. Third, the relationship needs to be restored, and full disclosure is necessary to sorting through problems and rebuilding. Fourth, the erring partner needs accountability, which is impossible without the spouse's knowledge of past failures. Nothing will ever be right until that sin is uncovered and rooted out.

When sin is not confessed in a marital relationship, the guilt will generally break up the relationship. It is certain that you won't have the oneness that couples really ought to have. Your marriage is a picture of Christ and the church, therefore great care should be given to maintaining it—or, if need be, restoring it.

Whatever your sin, if you have wronged another person, the right steps should be taken to make these wrongs right. It is the only way to completely rid yourself of the guilt that hounds you.

Forgiven and Cleansed!

Sometimes, we may remember something we did before we were saved and say, "I can't believe I did that. It was so wrong. I could kick myself." Sometimes the wrong act happened after salvation, and we think, "How can I sit here in church this morning and look so pious knowing what I did last week, last month, or last year? What I've done is horrible." And it is. It's terrible; it's wicked. But look at 1 John 1:9 again: *"If we confess our sins, he is faithful and just to forgive us our sins, and to cleanse us from all unrighteousness."* It tells us that when we confess our sins, the blood of Jesus Christ cleanses us from *all* sin—all unrighteousness. I don't have to carry my guilt anymore. I don't have to let it bother me anymore. I'm free from it.

You say, "But don't you ever think back?" Sure I do, sometimes. But, I just dump that past sin right back at the cross where I know it has already been forgiven. I don't have to carry the guilt for that sin any longer. It's forgiven, regardless of how rotten, once we have taken it to Jesus Christ.

When God saves a person, He picks up the broken pieces of a life, but He doesn't put them back together. He takes the worthless bits and creates something completely new—something beautiful. He wants to use this new life so that it has purpose and blessings. The problem is that people who are looking back can't see what is ahead of them. They are so focused on how bad they were that they don't go forward in their Christian growth and service. It's another dirty trick of the devil. Don't fall for it. Instead, see who God wants you to become and go forward. Never look back.

10

When You Feel Angry and Bitter

ECCLESIASTES 7:9

Be not hasty in thy spirit to be angry: for anger resteth in the bosom of fools.

Recently, my wife Mary and I finished a visit at the doctor's office and were heading out to the car. When we got to the parking lot, we heard a horn honking repeatedly. A man, as uptight as I've seen anybody in a long time, was laying on his horn, shaking his fist, and yelling. When I investigated to see what all the commotion was about, I realized that someone had pulled into the parking spot he was waiting for.

He finally opened his door and stood outside his truck. The other person, probably scared half to death, backed out, and the truck driver got his spot. Wow! I would venture to guess that the parking spot problem was not the only issue this guy had. Maybe he was dealing with a little bit of anger!

How about you? How do you respond when someone pulls in front of you on the highway or cuts in front of you and almost hits your bumper? What do you do when someone gossips about you? How do you react when your teenager refuses to obey? How you respond in irritating situations definitely has something to say about how you are managing your emotions. If anger is often your response—yelling, fuming, slamming doors, threatening—you need to learn to handle your emotions properly.

In the passage set out previously, the great preacher Solomon said, "*anger resteth in the bosom of fools.*" Fools are the ones who get caught up in anger. It's easy to look at the parking lot madman and think, "Yeah, he is definitely a fool." But somehow, when *we* get angry with people or at frustrating situations, we don't see ourselves as fools. In fact, we feel justified! "After all, I had every right to act in anger."

Did you? That's a question you need to ask yourself. Sometimes it *is* proper to respond with anger, and sometimes it isn't. It takes discernment to know the difference, and that is something the fool does not have much of. He generally defaults to anger.

Wise or Foolish?

The Bible says in Proverbs 19:11, "*The discretion of a man deferreth his anger; and it is his glory to pass over a transgression.*" The word *discretion* indicates a choice in the matter. We all have a choice concerning our emotions. I don't have to get angry, I don't have to yell, I don't have to fume and fight. I can act civilly. I have a choice, and so do you.

This verse also tells us that the man with discretion, the guy making right choices, will defer his anger. A wise man will choose not to get angry quickly, but he will weigh a matter out because he has the strength to control himself: "*He that is slow to anger is better than the mighty; and he that ruleth his spirit than he that taketh a city*" (Proverbs 16:32).

In Proverbs 14:29, we see again the contrast between the wise and the foolish man: "*He that is slow to wrath is of great understanding: but he that is hasty of spirit exalteth folly.*" The man who is slow to anger demonstrates that he has great understanding. The purpose of this chapter is to help you gain that kind of understanding—understanding about anger, about yourself—and to help you acquire some skill in managing your anger.

Learning how to make the choices that help you control your anger are lessons worth learning. They will help you to avoid relationship problems, health problems, and work problems, not to mention parking lot skirmishes! The verse we read at the beginning of this section says that "*it is his glory to pass over the transgression.*" It will be to your glory as well. You will be counted as a wise man rather than as a fool—in the sight of God and men.

We need to stop making excuses for our dispositions and our inclinations. Anger does not have to be an integral part of our daily emotional makeup. We *can* make wise choices concerning our emotions.

It's All Relative

Emotions are a God-given gift, not a curse. They are feelings that God has given to us for a purpose, so that we can be devout, faithful, loving, caring, and passionate. In other words, emotions enable us to be what God wants us to be. But we are inclined to think of some emotions as good and others as bad. For example, we tend to think of love as a good emotion and hate as a bad one. Is that true? Think about it. Love is good when the object of our love is God or people, but love is bad when the object of our love is this world's system. Hate is good when we abhor evil, but it is bad when we despise people.

Anger is one of those emotions we tend to think of as evil—because it causes us so much trouble—but anger itself is not sinful. The Bible says, "*Be ye angry, and sin not*" (Ephesians 4:26). We can see from this verse that it is possible to have anger without sinning. It is actually a good emotion when properly directed. It is the abuse of this emotion that causes sin. So, when is it okay to have anger and when is it not?

Good Anger, Bad Anger

There are times when anger is helpful. God intentionally designed us with this emotion to fulfill particular purposes in our lives. Anger is good, for example, when it helps us to interpret sinful behavior. In John 2, Jesus was angry when He drove the crooks out of the temple of God because they were exploiting temple worship as a mere means of profiting themselves financially. Though He was angry, He was completely in control of His emotions. He didn't pick up the first thing available and begin knocking moneychangers over the head. He deliberately made a whip of small cords to accomplish what He needed to do—run off the people abusing the house of God.

Anger can help us drive the sins out of our own lives too. I get disgusted and angry with myself when I don't live the way I know God wants me to. Paul expressed the same frustration with himself, *"For I know that in me (that is, in my flesh,) dwelleth no good thing: for to will is present with me; but how to perform that which is good I find not. For the good that I would I do not: but the evil which I would not, that I do. Now if I do that I would not, it is no more I that do it, but sin that dwelleth in me"* (Romans 7:18–20). Paul got so angry at his sinfulness that he finally exclaimed, *"O wretched man that I am! who shall deliver me from the body of this death?"* (Romans 7:24).

That's good anger. It drove Paul to the only Person who could help him live a holy life. The next verse says, *"I thank God through Jesus Christ our Lord"* (Romans 7:25). Paul turned to Christ to help him in his weakness, and in his later writings, we find Paul living a much more victorious life, dying to himself and walking in the Spirit. That's what anger is good for; it helps us change when we direct our anger toward sin.

Anger helps us fight off the devil, the wicked temptations of the world, and the sinful desires of the flesh. It helps us to better hate evil. We witness what anger does in others' lives—breaking up families, squandering potential, and destroying lives. When we see the heartbreak and turmoil it causes, it helps us to firmly resolve to spend time in prayer and Bible study and to go to church to hear the Word of God and draw strength from other Christians.

Anger is also good when it acts with the conscience as a warning signal. Have you ever found yourself in a situation like this? You foolishly hurt someone with unkind words or actions, and then immediately you felt angry with yourself. You wondered why you had been so idiotic, and you slapped yourself a few times. Your inner voice was judging you with anger. Usually, this self-judgment is constructive because it helps you analyze your behavior and your thinking processes so that you can change them or get the help you need to change.

Thank God He equipped us with this useful emotion. Without it, we would be more apt to remain in the sinful condition in which we were born.

Unfortunately, the same emotion that helps us avoid sin and change harmful patterns can also be the driving force behind some very sinful behaviors. When does anger itself become sinful? What kind of anger is sinful anger?

ANGER DIRECTED AT PEOPLE

Why is it that, given the same situation, two people can react in completely different ways—one remains in control while the other reacts with fury? The causes of anger can be very complex. They are usually based on feelings of failure, unrealistic beliefs about people and their motives, lack of problem-solving skills, and skewed perceptions about life in general. Couple any of those with behavior learned from a model, usually a parent, and you end up with someone who has difficulty tolerating the strain of everyday life without flying into a rage.

Oftentimes, people who react with unbridled anger do so because they believe other people are the cause of their inner turmoil. When this is the case, they attack people without really understanding the reasons themselves. They are simply angry people.

Regardless of the reasons, the Bible spells out plainly that the actions of these angry people are sinful. In fact, Proverbs 29:22 says they *abound* in transgression: *"An angry man stirreth up strife, and a furious man aboundeth in transgression."* Whatever the underlying causes of our anger, we do have a choice regarding what we do with it. Since it is our choice, God holds us accountable for anger that is intended to hurt another person.

You can try to justify the use of anger to hurt, perhaps defending yourself by blaming the other person for the way you feel, for your mistrust, for your sense of isolation, for any number of perceived offences, but no one has the power to make you angry. You choose to become angry, and you choose the actions that follow. The only thing you don't get to choose is the consequence that results from your sin. That's right, I called it sin.

I suppose it makes us feel better to believe that we are victims of our anger, but a skunk by any other name is still a skunk. You can put a ribbon around its neck; you can douse it in perfume, but when it wants to be a stinker, it will be a stinker! Call yourself a victim, point fingers, and assign blame. Give all the rationale you can think of, but anger used to hurt people is an improper use of that emotion; therefore, it is sinful.

ANGER ROOTED IN SELFISHNESS

"That was *my* parking space!" "*I* was expecting something better than this!" "Why didn't someone tell *me* about the change?" "Why won't you just do what *I* say?"

We want things our way. When things don't go our way we feel as if we have lost control, and our powerlessness makes us angry. What's worse is that if we do not have control, someone else *does*, and that makes us angrier! Relinquishing control means handing it over to someone else. Why should I do that? I have my rights.

We want control over our circumstances, control over our destinies, and the truth is we want control over other people. We want them to do what we want them to do, but they don't always cooperate. The very idea that we can't force people to conform to all our wants and wishes makes us feel very frustrated and angry.

Perhaps you've had an experience like this: you were in an office meeting discussing a problem. Suddenly, a light bulb came on; you had the perfect solution to the problem. It was a great idea, but the boss shot it down. No one ever seems to care when you have something to contribute, and you feel angry about it. The more you think about it, the angrier you get.

Picture yourself on a typical Sunday morning. You're ready to go, but your wife is not. You're thinking, "Sure we have five kids, but she knows what time we need to leave the house to be there on time." So you go to the car. You turn on the ignition and wait patiently—for a good ten or fifteen seconds—but still no family. So, in a very loving manner you lay on the horn and yell words of encouragement. "Hurry up! Come on!" Finally, they scurry out, some of the kids dragging their coats on the ground; your wife is carrying a couple of the little ones—almost dressed. She tosses the kids in and gets one foot in the door as you throw the car in reverse and take your foot off the brake. You're furious. You don't want to talk, and you don't want any talking in the car. "We're going to be late. Why can't she just do what I tell her to do?" is all you can think as you fume all the way to church.

Now, examine those situations. Why did you get upset when your expert opinion was overlooked? Was it because you were concerned for the good of the company or because your ego was deflated? Why were you angry that your wife didn't have the kids ready? Was it your concern for your family's spiritual condition, or was it the embarrassment or inconvenience being late would cause you?

Why do we get angry when things don't go our way? You can go back to the scenarios at the beginning of this section for the answer. Do you notice all the personal pronouns, the *I's, my's,* and *me's*? Our anger is sometimes—oftentimes—rooted in our own selfishness. All of us are selfish by nature, but self-centeredness is contrary to Scriptural mandates concerning our relationships. "*Be kindly affectioned one to another with brotherly love; in honour preferring one another*" (Romans 12:10). Plain and simple, when our anger is rooted in self, it is sinful no matter how frustrating our circumstances.

ANGER ROOTED IN PRIDE

"What? Ben got the promotion and the raise? How is that even possible? He's so young. He doesn't have enough experience to do that job. I am much better qualified."

Oh! That's a painful situation!

You wait anxiously to see if your husband likes your new hairstyle as much as you do. You feel a flutter in your stomach as you hear the front door swing open, and you take one last look in the mirror before you make your grand appearance into the living room. He takes one look and snorts, "How much did that cost?"

Ouch! That really hurt!

What do you do? You would probably do what most people do in either one of these situations—lash out like a grizzly.

It is dangerous to mess with a grizzly, especially a wounded one. In September last year, two men were hunting black bears in Montana near the Canadian border. One of the men mistakenly wounded a 400-pound grizzly and then tracked it into the thick cover. The grizzly bear attacked the shooter, but his hunting partner diverted his attention from the younger man. The grizzly turned to his new pursuit and took him down, killing him with crushing blows. Wounded animals are vicious. Their pain causes them to become aggressive, and instinctively, they attack anyone they perceive to be a threat.

Aren't we like that when we've been wounded? Your spouse yells, "Why didn't you make sure there was money in the account before you wrote that check? Now look what you've done! You've cost us more money!" That cutting remark caused a wound. Now you're angry. You're like the ferocious grizzly. It's time to attack. In your mind, the wound you sustained justifies your getting angry and striking back.

In truth, it was wrong for your spouse to yell at you, but does that give you the right to lash out in anger? If your spouse's actions were wrong, then returning hurt for hurt is also wrong. Now you're both wrong. Nothing was bettered. The situation is only made worse.

Now, think about *why* you retaliate. "Well, my spouse hurt me." That's it exactly. *You* were hurt. In these situations, it is our pride that gets wounded, and when our pride is wounded, it goes for blood.

It's your pride that says, "Okay, if that's the way you want it, I'm ready to fight." *"Only by pride cometh contention: but with the well advised is wisdom"* (Proverbs 13:10). I don't know if that verse could be any plainer: the *only* way contention occurs is when pride gets involved. *"Proud and haughty scorner is his name, who dealeth in proud wrath"* (Proverbs 21:24). Do you answer to that name? Do you strike back in anger? Anger that retaliates is sinful anger because it is rooted in pride, and Proverbs 16:5 uses some very strong language to describe God's viewpoint on this thing of pride: *"Every one that is proud in heart is an abomination to the LORD: though hand join in hand, he shall not be unpunished."*

ANGER THAT PREDOMINATES

Try to imagine what America would be like if we ceased all military operations, canned all intelligence personnel, dispensed with U.S. Customs and Border Protection, disbanded the Secret Service Agency, and halted all foreign diplomacy. How secure would you feel? If your mind produced terrifying images of invasion and attack, you would not be unjustified. We would leave ourselves completely vulnerable to any and every terrorist regime with a mind to impose on us its own political resolutions and strip us of the rights and freedoms we hold dear.

In Proverbs 25:28, the Bible uses a simile to illustrate the vulnerability of the man who cannot control his own emotions and impulses. It says, *"He that hath no rule over his own spirit is like a city that is broken down, and without walls."* All the cities in Bible times had walls around them for the protection of the people. The wall was their main means of defense against enemy infiltration or attack, just as ours is our military might.

If you often find yourself unable to control your angry impulses—you yell at your spouse or children, quarrel with coworkers, tell off business associates, get in a huff at waitresses, or occasionally kick your dog—your anger is controlling you. This should alarm you, because according to the Bible, you are wide open to satanic attack. In fact, you have probably experienced trouble, whether it be relational, spiritual, emotional, or even physical because you have left yourself without protection.

If our country was in the condition I mentioned earlier, without national defense, what would be our best course of action? Certainly the best option would *not* be inaction. Such a breech in security would require immediate measures to regain control and restore security.

That is the course of action I suggest for you as well. If your anger is controlling you, then you have relinquished control to the enemy. Anything that controls you besides God is sinful and must be deposed. God, who created you and redeemed you, is the only one who has the right to control your life, and you must take immediate measures to put God in His rightful place—Commander-in-Chief.

Anger can be handled in only two ways. There's the wrong way and there's the right way. Simple, right? "I wish it were," you say, "I've been battling anger issues for years, and I never seem to be able to get the victory." That tells me that you've probably been handling your anger the wrong way.

The Wrong Way

There are two traps people fall into when they become angry—both are defeating. I'm indebted to Dr. Jay Adams, a Christian counselor, who said these two things a few years ago in a seminar I attended. I've never forgotten them.

VENTING

The first wrong way to handle anger is blowing up. It could be called venting—blowing off steam. You can call it what you want to, but it can be disastrous.

Years ago, before the age of crockpots and microwaves, a lot of people used pressure cookers. My mom used one regularly. A pressure cooker does exactly what its name implies. It creates a lot of pressure causing things to cook more quickly. The pot is sealed so that steam builds inside, thus increasing the pressure. It is designed so that if the vent pipe gets plugged, or if for some other reason the pressure gets too high in the pot, the over pressure plug will blow, and with it comes the contents of the pan! (At least that's what the old ones used to do.)

That's the way some people handle their anger. They stay sealed up, allowing the pressure to build inside, and then POW! Like Mt.Vesuvius, they blow up, mad as fire, and here it all comes. Everything inside the "pot" blows out, burning the people who are close by.

Surprisingly, some psychiatrists agree that venting is a good way to handle your anger, so long as you don't blow up on people. I read one psychiatrist's Internet article in which he discussed diffusing anger. His advice to people who blow up easily is to go home and take out their anger on a soft pillow. He said, "Hit it, beat it, throw it, kick it, spit at it, do whatever feels good, but vent your anger on that pillow."

That's not the right way, nor is it the biblical way to handle your anger. I admit, it doesn't cause the disaster that venting on a person does, but it's just a useless exercise. Venting does nothing to resolve the problem at hand or change the wrong thinking that caused the anger to begin with. The anger will still be there when someone "plugs his vent pipe," and the angry person *will* blow.

When a pressure cooker blows there is no way to control what happens and who gets burned. If you handle your anger this way, you are not in control. You are like the city with broken down walls or the hasty fool Solomon described. If you say, "That's me. I vent on people," you need to recognize this is not a good way to handle your anger and take proper steps to control your temper.

CLAMMING UP

The second improper way of handling anger suggested by Dr. Adams is clamming up. It could be called internalizing.

Though we usually think of angry people as those who yell, argue, and punch walls, more often people handle their anger by internalizing. Rather than confront problems, they think it is easier to walk away and brush off the problem with, "I don't want to talk about it."

They often have a hard time even recognizing their anger, "Well, I'm not getting angry," they say, but they *are* getting angry. Instead of venting it toward others, they bury it. If this is how you handle anger, you may think you are keeping your true emotions to yourself, but the truth is that your anger does manifest itself outwardly in moodiness, loneliness, depression, relationship struggles, and a host of other problems. It shows on your face and it shows in your actions—you can't hide anger, and you can't bury it. Buried anger is still there eating away at you and sending down roots of bitterness into your heart.

Blowing up (venting) and clamming up (internalizing) are two ways you do not want to handle anger because neither resolves the anger. It just lingers on and on.

LINGERING ANGER TURNS TO BITTERNESS

When anger lingers on, it always turns to bitterness. When a person gets angry but doesn't deal with the issues as they arise, they fester. Usually, this person has many offences stockpiled because he is in the habit of venting or clamming up rather than resolving problems. Bitterness becomes a habit—part of who he is. He is filled with bitter thoughts. "He didn't have a right to do that to me," or "She shouldn't have talked to me that way." The bitter person usually has unresolved problems that go way back to childhood.

Maybe you are experiencing haunting memories. You remember what a parent, brother, sister, or some other person did, and it makes you angry every time you think about it. That's what the Bible calls the *"root of bitterness"* in Hebrews 12:15.

Look what Hebrews 12:15 says about that root of bitterness. *"Looking diligently lest any man fail of the grace of God; lest any root of bitterness springing up trouble you, and thereby many be defiled."* Who does the root of bitterness trouble? That's right, it troubles you.

Let's say that ten years ago a staff member said something that hurt me deeply, but because I never said anything about it to him, he doesn't even know that he offended me or that I hold ill feelings toward him. But the fact is I do. I stew over it all the time. "He shouldn't have said that to me. The way he treated me is infuriating!" Ten years later and I'm still stewing. Feelings of anger well up inside me every time I think about it. Now tell me, who is hurting because of the anger, the staff member or me? I am. It's my problem, not his.

HANDLING ANGER

The reason you still agonize over incidents from years gone by is that you have never dealt with the problem biblically. Ephesians 4:26 gives very explicit instructions on dealing with anger: *"Be ye angry, and sin not: let not the sun go down upon your wrath."* We are not to allow even one day to go by without taking care of the problem that caused our anger. The responsibility of doing so rests upon the angered one.

Have you ever gone to bed angry? I have. Anger makes a very poor bedfellow. After all the tossing and turning, sleep may come, but when you wake up, the first thing that pops into your consciousness is the unresolved issue. You may even awaken with feelings of emptiness, guilt or bitterness. The problem is still there. It will always be there—until you go to the person who angered you and work things out. So, how do you do that? How do we handle anger in a biblical way?

The Right Way

Anger cannot be allowed to fester. Therefore, you must meet this problem head on and deal with it according to the Scriptures. You may have a lot of anger built up inside you—maybe toward many people. Begin with the issues that cause you the most inner conflict, or begin with your most important relationships. Ask God for wisdom and guidance, but by all means stand up and fight against this destructive enemy.

PUT OFF ANGER

Make the decision to deal with your own issues. The Bible says in Ephesians 4:31, *"Let all bitterness, and wrath, and anger, and clamour, and evil speaking, be put away from you, with all malice."* In Colossians 3:8, Paul writes, *"But now ye also put off all these; anger, wrath, malice, blasphemy, filthy communication out of your mouth."* Put them off. Get rid of them.

First, recognize that you have sinned in clinging to your anger. When God looks at the real you, He looks into your heart. What He wants to find is the likeness of His Son—love, joy, peace, longsuffering, gentleness, goodness, faith, meekness, and temperance—but when He finds bitterness, anger, and all sorts of malice instead, He is grieved and displeased. To have a right relationship with Him, you must get your heart right. Confess to the Lord that you have disobeyed His Word regarding how He has directed you to manage your emotions and guard your heart. Make a commitment that you are *not* going to continue harboring ill feelings and keeping track of past wrongs. Just as I would take off my coat, I put off anger. It's a decision of the will.

Unfortunately, we are sinful creatures, and we live in a sinful world with other sinful people; therefore, we will all face actions or remarks that incite feelings of anger. When those offences come, God wants us to deal with them biblically. What does the Bible tell us to do when we have an offense that must be resolved?

GO

"Moreover if thy brother shall trespass against thee, go and tell him his fault between thee and him alone: if he shall hear thee, thou hast gained thy brother" (Matthew 18:15). As the offended party, it's my responsibility to go to the offender and say, "I know you probably didn't mean this..." or "You may not have known you did this, but this thing still bothers me." Go to the offender in the right spirit and tell him what he did. Give him a chance to explain his point of view or to offer an apology.

He may respond well. He may not, but at least you did your part to clear the air. If you have been stockpiling, and you have more than one issue to talk over, you might start with one—maybe the one you feel to be the most important.

Before you go, prepare to handle the situation in a godly manner.

GIVE A SOFT ANSWER

Don't fight fire with fire. The Bible says in Proverbs 15:1, *"A soft answer turneth away wrath: but grievous words stir up anger."* Before you ever go to someone to handle a relationship problem, you must decide how you will speak and the words you will use. Talking about these problems can be very emotional, and before you know it, the conversation can erupt into a shouting match. If you are yelling, you are not communicating; therefore, nothing will be accomplished.

Follow these guidelines for more effective communication:

1. Resolve to speak in a civil tone, no matter how the other person speaks.
2. Use only words that are kind, not grievous.
3. Be careful not to attack the person; instead attack the problem. Never resort to insults or name-calling that will put the other person on the defensive.
4. Redirect your energy to solving your problem. Honestly, if we used the energy that we use to attack each other to attack the problem instead, we would have much better relationships.

Taking this "soft" approach will do just what the Bible says. It will diffuse your anger and the other person's. By the way, notice that you *should* respond with an answer. It's not a matter of clamming up and internalizing. It's a matter of communicating effectively.

ACT RATHER THAN REACT

"The heart of the righteous studieth to answer: but the mouth of the wicked poureth out evil things" (Proverbs 15:28). A righteous person will study. In other words, he will think before he speaks. He will put his brain in gear before he puts his tongue in motion. Before you speak, you want to ask yourself, "Do I really know what has happened? Do I understand the other person's point of view? What is God trying to help me to see?"

Making erroneous assumptions is one of the common causes of anger. We assume that we know what the other person meant. We assume we know what he was thinking in a given situation. We assume we know the motives behind his actions.

Notice the emphasis in Proverbs 18:13 and 15: *"He that answereth a matter before he heareth it, it is folly and shame unto him… The heart of the prudent getteth knowledge; and the ear of the wise seeketh knowledge."* The emphasis is on hearing before speaking. Be ready to listen to the person who made you angry.

If you will listen, you may gather information that will help you to better evaluate and understand the problem. When we take the time to listen, we often find that we misunderstood the situation to begin with, or sometimes we find out that we contributed to the problem ourselves. If so, acknowledge any part you may have had in the conflict and ask for forgiveness. Sometimes just hearing the other side of an issue is enough to free you of your anger. Get to the bottom of a problem instead of simply spouting off.

LET SOME THINGS GO

Proverbs 20:3 is a key verse, *"It is an honour for a man to cease from strife: but every fool will be meddling."* The next time somebody in the office really irritates you to no end, just keep in mind, it's an honor if you can just back off. This does not mean internalizing the anger. It means not getting angry at all. It means letting it go because some things are just not worth getting angry over. You don't have to fight. You don't have to hold out for your way. You don't have to demand your rights. You don't have to defend yourself. Just forgive him and go on. God says it's an honor. It's not easy, but it is honorable when you can develop the kind of disposition that does not get offended over every little thing.

GIVE GOD CONTROL

You can develop this kind of disposition, but it takes the Holy Spirit producing His fruit in your life to counter the proclivity of your flesh toward anger, bitterness, and malice. In chapter 8, we discussed our need to be filled with the Spirit to battle our fleshly desires. This filling is every bit as needful when we are trying to conquer our angry disposition and our fleshly responses to the irritations we encounter. Just as dying to yourself is important to controlling your desires, it is also important to controlling your anger. If you have problems with anger, you may want to go back and reread that section of chapter 8 and begin today seeking His filling and walking in Him.

The application is different, but walking in the Spirit still involves making choices whether you are battling lust or anger. You have a choice to walk in the flesh or to walk in the Spirit. When your ten-year-old has piled everything in his closet instead of cleaning his room, and you feel rage building because this is the fifth day in a row you have had to deal with the same kind of irresponsibility, you have a choice to make. You can walk in the flesh, or you can walk in the Spirit. The parent who is walking in the flesh will go snatch that kid from the television and yell at him all the way to his bedroom where the real fireworks begin. The parent who is walking in the Spirit will stop and pray, "Lord, help me to have the wisdom to handle this situation the way You want me to handle it. Help me to mete out the punishment that will help this boy develop good character. Help me not to act in anger."

Remember, you are not likely to make the right choices on your own. You need God's help every day, every moment. If you go into this fight alone, you will not prevail. Think of all the times Israel charged into battle without God on their side—either because of their sin or self-reliance. Those were always ugly defeats. But when they obeyed the Lord and looked to Him for their strength, God did amazing miracles to give them the victory. You want God on your side, friend. Stick to Him as closely as you possibly can throughout this battle, and watch Him give the victory.

Conclusion

Anger is a God-given emotion. Let the Lord use good anger to help you recognize evil, despise it, and fight off the temptations that come your way. Get rid of sinful anger daily—before the sun goes down. Don't allow it to embitter you. And never use sinful anger against people.

If you are struggling with anger, you have a long road ahead of you, but don't give up. Take it one day at a time, one step at a time, until you have more victories than defeats. You can win this fight with God's help. He is in the heart-changing business, and He will change yours if you will let Him. Give Him control of the battle every day, and continue to fight the good fight.

11

When You Feel Burned Out

I KINGS 18:37

Hear me, O Lord, hear me, that this people may know that thou art the Lord God, and that thou hast turned their heart back again.

All the Israelites waited on Mount Carmel with eager anticipation. Everyone likes an exciting competition, and thousands had turned out that day to see the contest of the century. In one corner, we have the prophet, Elijah, representing the only true God of Heaven, and in the other corner, the prophets of Baal, representing their god crafted from stone by human hands.

We have to back up a little to lay some groundwork for this thrilling event. King Ahab was the king of Israel at this time. When he came to power, it was bad news for the nation. He had done more evil than all the other kings before him, even Jeroboam, whose sins he followed. If that wasn't enough, he took wicked Jezebel to be his wife and worshipped her god Baal.

God had seen enough and sent his man Elijah to tell Ahab that He was sending three years of drought because of Ahab's wickedness. Since Ahab was always looking at life through sin's distorted lenses, he believed Elijah to be the cause of Israel's troubles. Of course, that was a little easier to believe than the real truth, which would cast him as the villain.

This is where the contest begins—with the finger pointing. After three long years with no rain, not even a drop of dew, Elijah appeared before the king again. Ahab, just to make sure that people weren't blaming him for this mess, jumped up, and with a dramatic sweep of his hand toward Elijah, he yelled in a sarcastic tone, "Could this be the troublemaker Elijah who has caused Israel's woes?"

Elijah shot back boldly, "You and your fathers have caused Israel this trouble in forsaking your God and following Baal, but if you would care to have a contest to find out which God you should follow, round up your 850 wicked prophets and all the people of Israel and meet me on Mount Carmel."

The false doctrine that proliferated about Baal was that he controlled all the elements of the world. His worshippers believed it was he who sent the rain and the lightning. To challenge this nonsense, Elijah arranged for them to display Baal's strong suit, raining down fire from Heaven. Surely, this would be no problem for the one who controlled the lightning. Each side prepared an identical offering. Whoever sent fire to burn up the sacrifice would be declared the winner—the one and only true God.

The prophets of Baal put on quite a show, leaping on the altar and crying and cutting themselves while Elijah made jokes about their god. Evening arrived, but there was still no answer.

Now it was Elijah's turn. Not to be outdone by the showmanship of Baal's prophets, Elijah put on a show of his own, commanding that twelve barrels of water be poured on his sacrifice, just in case there were any that would doubt that the God of Heaven was the one who performed the miracle they were about to see. Twelve barrels might have been all the water left in Israel's depleting water supply, but Elijah had faith that God would give them the water they needed so desperately.

Elijah then called on God. "*And it came to pass at the time of the offering of the evening sacrifice, that Elijah the prophet came near, and said, Lord God of Abraham, Isaac, and of Israel, let it be known this day that thou art God in Israel, and that I am thy servant, and that I have done all these things at thy word. Hear me, O Lord, hear me, that this people may know that thou art the Lord God, and that thou hast turned their heart back again*" (1 Kings 18:36–37).

Now it was God's turn. "*Then the fire of the Lord fell, and consumed the burnt sacrifice, and the wood, and the stones, and the dust, and licked up the water that was in the trench. And when all the people saw it, they fell on their faces: and they said, The Lord, he is the God; the Lord, he is the God. And Elijah said unto them, Take the prophets of Baal; let not one of them escape. And they took them: and Elijah brought them down to the brook Kishon, and slew them there. And Elijah said unto Ahab, Get thee up, eat and drink; for there is a sound of abundance of rain*" (1 Kings 18:38–41).

Elijah had just experienced a great victory, but as is often the case after triumph, he was physically and emotionally spent. After the mountaintop comes the valley, which made Elijah a prime candidate for what we might call burnout.

The term *burnout* was coined to describe the condition of a person who is mentally, physically, emotionally, and oftentimes spiritually exhausted. These feelings often arise because of inadequacy at having failed to achieve his desired goals or a certain level of success.

Besides the stress of our own expectations, we experience cultural stress in our fast-paced society with all its challenges and demands. In the mid-nineteenth century, more people lived on farms than in cities. Now it is the opposite. In the early twentieth century, most people were born, married, and died in their same community. In today's mobile society, many move several times. Friends change, surroundings change, jobs change, and the pressures usually increase. These changes have impacted society as a whole.

Even advances in medicine have brought about a new phenomenon in society—midlife crisis. Just a century ago, the life expectancy for men was 48 years; for women, 51. The Centers for Disease Control and Prevention reported in November 2004 that the life expectancy for men is 74.5 years; for women, 79.9. This change has created new subcultures in America, one being mid-lifers, people who have years ahead of them, but have accomplished most of what they set out to do—build a career, raise a family, procure financial security. They look back and question if they have accomplished anything meaningful and look ahead with fear at the uncertainty that lies before them.

Jim Conway, in his book *Men in Midlife Crisis*, said, "The midlife crisis is a time of high risk for marriages. It's a time for possible career disruption and extramarital affairs. There's depression, anger, frustration and rebellion. The crisis is a pervasive thing that seems to affect not only the physical but the social, cultural, spiritual, and occupational expressions of a man's life. Frustration, stress, crisis all help to make up the recent phenomenon we have labeled 'burnout.'"

Perhaps you have experienced some of these feelings. This melancholia could be related to your job, marriage or other family relationships, and/or goals. Things just didn't seem to turn out exactly as you imagined they would—your achievements don't seem as lofty as your dreams were, but now what do you do? It's too late to start over. Frustrated with life, you feel like getting on a plane to go...anywhere.

Although Alexander wasn't suffering from burnout, (he was probably no more than seven or eight years old), in the book *Alexander and the Terrible, Horrible, No Good, Very Bad Day*, he seems to relate to this need to escape. He elucidates for us: "I went to sleep with gum in my mouth and now there's gum in my hair, and when I got out of bed this morning I tripped on a skateboard and, by mistake, dropped my sweater in the sink while the water was running and I could tell it was going to be a terrible, horrible, no good, very bad day."

After a terrible day at school, a horrible visit to the dentist, and a no-good stop at the shoe store, Alexander slumps in his chair at the supper table, and continues his account. "There was lima beans for dinner (I hate lima beans), there was kissing on TV (I hate kissing), my bath was too hot and I got soap in my eyes, and my marble went down the drain, and I had to wear my railroad train pajamas (I hate railroad train pajamas). When I went to bed, Nick took back the pillow that he said I could keep, my Mickey Mouse nightlight burned out and I bit my tongue, and the cat wants to sleep with Anthony, not me. It has been a terrible, horrible, no good, very bad day."

At the end of the book, it's no wonder that Alexander said, "I think I'll move to Australia." Even as a little kid, he just wanted to get away from it all. Elijah came to that place in his life as well—he wanted to bolt.

He had just experienced a great victory for his God. When all the people saw God's mighty power, they literally fell on their faces and proclaimed the Lord to be God. Everyone rejoiced, except Ahab. Elijah had humiliated him and made a mockery of his worship. He was angry, to say the least!

Ahab did what he normally did when things didn't go his way. He went home and cried to Jezebel, who also did what she normally did when things didn't go her way. She flew into a violent rage (maybe you can see why people don't name their baby girls Jezebel). "*Then Jezebel sent a messenger unto Elijah, saying, So let the gods do to me, and more also, if I make not thy life as the life of one of them by to morrow about this time*" (1 Kings 19:2). In other words, she promised to kill him.

What did Elijah do? He knew Jezebel was wicked enough to make good on her threat—he ran! "*And when he saw that, he arose, and went for his life, and came to Beersheba, which belongeth to Judah, and left his servant there. But he himself went a day's journey into the wilderness, and came and sat down under a juniper tree: and he requested for himself that he might die; and said, It is enough; now, O Lord, take away my life; for I am not better than my fathers*" (1 Kings 19:3–4).

The Bible says in James 5:17 that Elijah "*was a man subject to like passions as we are.*" He felt fear. He got discouraged. He suffered burnout, just as we do.

Now, he was at an all-time low. God had won the victory in an amazing display of power, and maybe Elijah thought he was done—no more fighting, no more conflict, no more scrapes—but now here he was, in another big one. And worse yet, this one was a personal crisis. Jezebel was after *his* blood!

After all the fighting he had already done, running for his life was more than he could take. Maybe he even felt as though God had turned on him at this point, and he gave up. He thought, "God, You show me a miracle one day, and now You've got me on the run. I don't want to do this anymore. I can't take the constant struggle. Go ahead and take my life." Elijah was experiencing absolute burnout.

It's like going to church on Sunday and getting that spiritual lift you need. Everything is wonderful—that is, until you come up against the "real world" on Monday. You're faced, once again with the daily grind and the struggles of work and family life. You feel like you can't meet the demands constantly placed on you, and though you are giving it your best shot, you feel like no one recognizes or appreciates what you do. Sometimes you wonder if it's really worth the effort.

Dear reader, if you are struggling with these types of feelings, you are in a vulnerable place. Be careful. Don't make the same mistakes Elijah made while he was in this state of depletion. Read the following features of burnout. If you recognize yourself in these features, it is probably time to step back and reevaluate your life.

Don't Isolate Yourself

Notice one mistake that Elijah made. "*And when he saw that, he arose, and went for his life, and came to Beersheba, which belongeth to Judah, and left his servant there. But he himself went a day's journey into the wilderness, and came and sat down under a juniper tree.*" Elijah separated himself from the one who could have encouraged, helped, and strengthened him. Elijah isolated himself during his burnout.

Oftentimes, alone is a dangerous place to be. Right when we need a friend, a counselor, or someone to lift us up, we withdraw instead of getting the help we need. If you are like me, you might say, "I'll deal with this on my own. I don't want to hear advice because I really don't want to know the truth. I just don't want to face up to my problems right now. I'd rather hibernate for a while." Are you cutting yourself off from your friends and family when you really need them most?

Sometimes, just expressing your feelings to a listening ear can help. "But that's part of the problem," you say, "No one really cares." Feeling alone and underappreciated is a sign of burnout. All your focus is inward—and selfish, I might add.

Maybe with your inward focus, you are not looking at things realistically. Elijah withdrew from society when, in reality, it was only two people who were against him. Everyone else had turned back to the Lord. Later God reminded Elijah that he wasn't alone, that there were still 7,000 who had never bowed their knee to Baal. You're not alone either. You just feel alone right now, and feelings are never a good basis for judging reality.

You might be surprised at the support you'd find if you tried talking to someone. Come out of your self-imposed cocoon and get the help you need when you feel drained and defeated.

Be Careful about Setting Expectations

I'm surmising, but maybe the reason Elijah felt the way he did was that his expectations and dreams of success were not fulfilled. I think he had an idea of how things were going to go after this amazing victory in Israel. This great revival, no doubt, was something he had envisioned for a very long time. Maybe it went something like this: After God displayed His mighty power, Ahab would repent of his wickedness, turn back to God, and lead the nation to follow the Lord. But that's not what happened. Instead, Ahab and Jezebel became angry and more defiant than ever. This is not the way it was supposed to turn out, at least not in Elijah's mind.

Maybe he thought this triumph would immediately change everything about his life. Maybe he thought that from that point on, he would live "happily ever after," serving his God with no more cares and woes. I dare say that death threats were not part of his expectations.

Do you ever get an idea of how God is supposed to answer your prayers or order your life? Have you ever found yourself feeling defeated because God did not follow your script? Sometimes we build up expectations that are not God's expectations, outcomes that are not even part of God's plan.

Take that as a warning: If you're going after your goals and your dreams, and you're determined to achieve them come what may, you may be running ahead of God and setting yourself up for disappointment. Be careful; shattered dreams often lead people to a life of cynicism.

Years ago, while we were averaging about four hundred people in Sunday school at Fairfax Baptist Temple, we decided to launch out and set a goal of having a thousand people in attendance at our anniversary Sunday.

I had been fasting and praying daily for a long time, "Lord, we want 1,000 people." The big day finally came, and we had 963 people in the morning service. I was so discouraged. We only had 963 people, and I felt defeated. Do you know why? Because *my* goal wasn't fulfilled, because God hadn't worked things exactly according to my plan. Looking at the missed goal instead of the achievement, I lost sight of what an amazing work God had done.

When I got home, I didn't want anyone around me. I had a pity party, thinking about how things hadn't worked out. Then it struck me that God had given us over twice as many people in church as we normally had, and a number of those people were born into God's family. We had had an exciting service—a wonderful service—people filled chairs all over the auditorium. But all I had been able to think about was that I had fallen short of my goal.

I learned from that. My goal doesn't matter if it's not God's goal. My job and your job is *not* to determine the criteria for success. Our job is to do God's will, and then say, "Wow, God! Look what You did."

You may not make the goal or obtain that position you wanted, but that doesn't mean you have failed. God may not have answered your prayer exactly the way you wanted Him to, but that doesn't mean God failed. God used Elijah's life exactly the way He wanted to, but He wasn't finished. He was still working. He is still working in your life too. So, you can't get defeated. You can't quit. There is still more God wants you to do.

Consider Your Options

Another symptom of burnout is a feeling of helplessness. Trying to cope with the pressures and struggles, you sometimes develop tunnel vision. You look around at your problems and feel as if you have no options.

For example, Jake feels trapped and ready to throw in the towel. He has a wife and kids to provide for, but not enough money coming in. As it is, he leaves early in the morning and gets home late at night. Now, the boss is pressuring him to take on more responsibility without more pay. More responsibility means more time at work and less time with the family. He feels guilty already because he's not spending enough time on his relationships, but he just doesn't see any way out. He has to keep this job.

Actually, Jake has options, but he has been running on the same hamster wheel so long, he can't see anything else. He just keeps running and running and running.

Elijah appeared to be in the same situation. He responded to the stress in his life without stopping to consider that he might have other options. There is no indication in Scripture that Elijah even stopped to ask God what he should do when his life was imperiled. He felt his only option was to run, but when he was completely spent, it seemed that giving up was the only way out.

Friend, if you just keep going, you will find yourself where Elijah was—completely spent and looking for a way out. The point is that there are usually many options from which we can choose to alleviate our pressure, but we just haven't stopped running long enough to see what God wants us to do. Sometimes we have to stop and prayerfully evaluate our lives and make adjustments where needed.

Don't Let Yourself Get Physically Depleted

It may be that the root cause of your feelings of burnout is simply fatigue. When you push your body beyond what God intended it to do, it is easy to feel as though you just can't go on. The simple fact is that you feel as if you have nothing left to give, because you don't. You say, "I just have too many demands on me to slow down and get some rest." Sure, you have stress, but the stress that drives you to keep going is also a huge contributor to the physical strain you feel. Stress takes its toll on us physically. You may think you have the will to keep pushing through the exhaustion, but God did not intend for you to live that way. He made provision for rest. We are the ones who ignore the warnings that God built into our bodies.

Consider just the physical strain Elijah's body had been through, never mind the emotional and mental strain. The job of executing 450 prophets of Baal had been grueling enough by itself, but after a day's journey without rest, Elijah was completely drained. That's when he reached the breaking point and lost all desire to live.

There comes a breaking point, friend. Physical exhaustion is one of the signals that something has to change.

What to Do When You Feel Burnout Coming

What do you do when you get to the end of your rope? Is there any hope when you get burned out on life? The answer is yes. There are solutions.

1. Address any physical needs that you may have. Notice what God does for Elijah in 1 Kings 19:5, *"And as he lay and slept under a juniper tree, behold, then an angel touched him, and said unto him, Arise and eat. And he looked, and, behold, there was a cake baken on the coals, and a cruse of water at his head. And he did eat and drink, and laid him down again. And the angel of the LORD came again the second time, and touched him, and said, Arise and eat; because the journey is too great for thee."* The angel said, "Get up and eat." In other words, take care of yourself physically.

Whatever strain you are experiencing at home, work, or school is only compounded by allowing yourself to get worn out physically. It's a vicious cycle. You may just need to separate yourself for a time to rest and pray, as Jesus often did. Someone put it this way: "Either you come apart and rest for awhile, or you may just come apart." Give yourself a break. Take vacation time if you have it. Get a few days away for a change of pace. Enjoy life a little bit, and smell the roses.

When you feel the pressure mounting, it is often due to many little things that you are neglecting. Your physical well-being is likely one of the things you are not tending to properly. Take care of yourself. First of all, get the sleep you need. That's hard to do sometimes, but it's still worth working on. Exercise to help you think clearly and release some of the pressure you've built up.

Be assured of God's care and concern. In verse 7, the Bible says, *"And the angel of the LORD came again the second time, and touched him, and said, Arise and eat; because the journey is too great for thee."* Did you catch that? God Himself dispatched the angel to help Elijah. Though Elijah had an episode of weakness and lapse in faith, God did not turn His back on Elijah. It was at that low point that God showed His tender care for His weak child.

I look at that and think it is wonderful to know that our great God in Heaven cares even about food and water. My Heavenly Father watches over me. From the Bible, I know with assurance that He does! You ought to think on that when you feel yourself giving in to the pressures and stresses in your life. God cares about me, and He cares about you. He's interested in our lives.

2. Spend time in God's Word. *"And he* [Elijah] *came thither unto a cave, and lodged there; and, behold, the word of the LORD came to him, and he said unto him, What doest thou here, Elijah?"* (1 Kings 19:9). None of us today will hear the audible voice of God like Elijah did, but we have God's Holy Word, the Bible. When you get a little down or discouraged, get into the Bible. When you feel like the pressures of life are weighing upon you, get into His Word. There, you will find His wisdom and answers for your problems. You will find comfort and strength to pick you up when you are down. Take time to listen to the still, small voice of God! He's still speaking today.

Oftentimes, He brings the pressures and the troubles so that we will turn to Him. Turn to the right place, friend. Turn to Him.

3. Look at your situation from a heavenly perspective. That's what God showed Elijah. Notice Elijah's perspective in verse 10: *"And he said, I have been very jealous for the LORD God of hosts: for the children of Israel have forsaken thy covenant, thrown down thine altars, and slain thy prophets with the sword; and I, even I only, am left; and they seek my life, to take it away."* His perspective was distorted by his own expectations. He expected Ahab to repent and turn back to worshipping Jehovah, but God didn't do what Elijah had expected. Elijah was sorely disappointed, and felt all alone, but that was only his perception. It wasn't the truth.

God sent Elijah up on top of Mount Horeb, the mount of God, to get a new perspective, a heavenly perspective, if you will. *"And he said, Go forth, and stand upon the mount before the LORD. And, behold, the LORD passed by, and a great and strong wind rent the mountains, and brake in pieces the rocks before the LORD; but the LORD was not in the wind: and after the wind an earthquake; but the LORD was not in the earthquake: And after the earthquake a fire; but the LORD was not in the fire: and after the fire a still small voice"* (1 Kings 19:11–12).

God taught Elijah an invaluable lesson that day. In essence He said, "Elijah, you can't put Me in a box. I don't always work the way you think I will, but I am working." God asked Elijah why he had come there, and then He showed him a great display in the wind, and the earthquake and the fire, as if to say, "Is this what you came to see?" But God was in none of it.

Then, after the roaring of the wind, and the rumbling of the earthquake, and the hissing of the fire came a stillness, a deafening quiet, in contrast to all the clamor of that ominous display, and Elijah heard the still, small voice. God taught Elijah, "Sometimes I do My work in a quiet way, in a way that is barely perceptible to you, but I am doing My work nonetheless. Just trust Me."

That's what you need to do. When you feel alone, exhausted, disappointed, and ready to give up, stop looking for your expectations to materialize in a glorious display of God's power, and trust Him. Listen for the still, small voice. Look for the unseen hand. Understand that He is still working.

4. Find out what it is God wants you to do. "*And the LORD said unto him, Go, return on thy way to the wilderness of Damascus: and when thou comest, anoint Hazael to be king over Syria: And Jehu the son of Nimshi shalt thou anoint to be king over Israel: and Elisha the son of Shaphat of Abelmeholah shalt thou anoint to be prophet in thy room*" (1 Kings 19:15–16).

After God finally got Elijah's attention, He then sent Elijah to go back and do the work that he was supposed to be doing to begin with. God was working in His own way, and each of these men—Hazael, Jehu, and Elisha—had his own role to play in what God would do in the nation of Israel. Eventually Elijah would turn over his mantle—a symbol of authority—to Elisha who would become a great prophet of God as well. Elijah still had work to do. He still had people to invest in.

Maybe you need to make some midcourse adjustments, but you still have work to do. You need to get alone with God to reevaluate your life and find out what that work is—not what you think you should be doing, not what you always dreamed you would do—but find out what God wants to do through you. Get His perspective on your life. Ask Him to direct you. Search His Word. Then, like Elijah, get back where you belong to do the work He wants you to do—nothing more, nothing less.

Conclusion

If you're experiencing the feelings we discussed, burnout may be just around the corner. Make the adjustments necessary now to avoid burnout.

If you are already there, share your burden with someone else. Get spiritual help from your pastor, but don't isolate yourself.

When a believer burns out, it's because his own human resources have finally been exhausted. He has tried everything he knows to do in his own strength. That's when you get into trouble—when you're controlling your life rather than letting God have control. When you get overwhelmed by life, when you're feeling burnt out, when everything seems too much to handle, it is nothing more than the clamor of the wind, the earthquake, and the fire—a wake-up call from Heaven, God's working in your life. He's getting your attention just as He got Elijah's.

God could have stopped Elijah dead in his tracks the moment he began to run. He could have said, "Hold on there, Elijah. I still have work here for you." But He didn't do that. He let Elijah run. He let him feel isolated and disappointed and spent. He let him get to the end of his rope. Why? Is God cruel? Does He not care that we hurt? You can answer that for yourself. Did God turn His back on Elijah at his very lowest point? No, on the contrary, He showed abundant mercy and tender care.

Would Elijah have listened to God's instructions in his petulant condition? Probably not. God got Elijah's attention, taught him what he needed to understand, and then—when Elijah was ready to hear—He told him what He wanted him to do.

Time and again, God has worked that way when I needed encouragement. I am so thankful for God's patient hand in my life. He still has work for me to do. I refuse to concede defeat. I refuse to quit. I refuse to curl up and die.

For ten years, until she passed away shortly after her 100th birthday, I fixed my mother-in-law's breakfast every morning. One morning, she was up a little earlier than usual. When I walked in about 6:30, she was standing at her typewriter because she couldn't get up on her own if she sat down. Her 94-year-old her hands were all curled up with arthritis. So, she stood there typing with one finger.

I came in and said, "Mom, what are you doing typing a letter so early this morning?"

She said, "I have so much to do today, I just had to get an early start on it."

I thought, "Ninety-four years of age—that's the zest you need in life." Even when your body is failing, don't give up. Keep pressing on. There's a job to do for the Lord.

He has work for you to do too, friend. Don't wave the white flag. Get up as Elijah did, make the adjustments you need to make, and go on for God.

12

When You Hear the "C" Word

PSALM 103:1–10

Bless the LORD, O my soul: and all that is within me, bless his holy name. Bless the LORD, O my soul, and forget not all his benefits: Who forgiveth all thine iniquities; who healeth all thy diseases; Who redeemeth thy life from destruction; who crowneth thee with lovingkindness and tender mercies: Who satisfieth thy mouth with good things; so that thy youth is renewed like the eagle's. The LORD executeth righteousness and judgment for all that are oppressed. He made known his ways unto Moses, his acts unto the children of Israel. The LORD is merciful and gracious, slow to anger, and plenteous in mercy. He will not always chide: neither will he keep his anger for ever. He hath not dealt with us after our sins; nor rewarded us according to our iniquities.

My Story

When I was about thirty-three years old, I had a little problem with my foot, and I was referred to a dermatologist. The foot turned out okay, but as the dermatologist was examining it, he noticed a mole on the back of my calf.

"I'd better biopsy that because it could be cancer," he told me.

"Doc, you don't understand," I said smiling, confidently, "I don't *do* cancer! I think you would be wasting your time, but if you think it best, go ahead and cut it off."

As I assumed he would, the dermatologist called me a week later and said everything was fine. I didn't have any cancer.

After my annual physical in the fall of 2006, my primary physician said something that took me back to my foot experience thirty years before. He told me that I needed to go see a urologist to get a second opinion regarding my prostate. The doctor wanted him to check for cancer.

I knew a little bit about prostate cancer because my dad and my younger brother both had it at one point. Since I knew I was genetically predisposed to it, I had done a little research, and I asked my doctor what my Prostate Specific Antigen (PSA) number was. It was normal for someone my age. Regardless, my doctor thought it best to get the opinion of a urologist.

Again, I figured this would be an exercise in futility since "I don't *do* cancer." My brother had told me the biopsy was as bad as the surgery, and I didn't want to waste my time doing a painful test just to find out that everything was fine. So I waited before going to see the urologist. I wasn't sure I wanted to go at all, but I knew that I had to face my primary physician for my annual physical again. So after ten months of putting it off, I reluctantly went and had the biopsy done.

After my biopsy, the doctor came out and told my wife, "I have done hundreds, even thousands, of these surgeries, and although I haven't heard back from the lab yet, I am confident there is absolutely nothing to be concerned about."

She was relieved, and I have to admit that I was relieved as well. I was scheduled to go back a week later to get my report. As six days ticked by, I thought, "This is just another waste of time. I'm going to have to leave work and wait in the waiting room just to find out what I already know—I'm fine."

I called the doctor's office to cancel my appointment, but the receptionist surprised me. "Sir," she said, "I don't think you can do that."

"Well, is there any chance you could get the doctor on the phone?" I asked. "Maybe he can tell me over the phone what the results are. That would save both of us a lot of time."

She paused a moment and said, "I'll check." Then she returned to the phone to say, "No, he said that he wants to see you in his office tomorrow."

Baffled and reluctant, I went. As I sat in his office, he looked across his desk and said, "Mr. Calvert, you have cancer, and you have a lot of it. Every piece of biopsy we took showed positive for cancer. I recommend you do something about it immediately."

My mind began a frenzied search. It was thumbing through all the Scriptures that I had ever memorized and flipping through every book I had read on Christian living. "Okay," I thought as I took inventory, "what is a Christian supposed to do when he hears the 'C' word?" Personally, I had always reserved that word for others.

The doctor wanted to give me a shot right then and put me on some pills to get me prepared for surgery the next week. Normally, when I need to have a procedure done, I am ready to get it over with immediately, but he told me the recovery could take several weeks. I knew that wouldn't work because Christmas was in a few days, and in January, we had planned to take our very first cruise. I definitely didn't want to interfere with that!

When I arrived home, I casually walked inside and chatted with Mary, as is my habit at the end of a workday. We were eating dinner when she asked, "By the way, how did it go at the doctor's office?"

"Oh," I said as matter-of-factly as I possibly I could, "he told me I have cancer."

"What?" she questioned, thinking, because of my manner, that I was joking, but when I finally convinced her, we had much to discuss.

Before I decided how to proceed I wanted to get a second opinion. I called a good friend from our church, a doctor who had a background in oncology. My friend got me an appointment with the best urologist he knew—the same afternoon! This urologist explained all my options but recommended a radical prostatectomy, which I had done on February 26, 2007. For those of you keeping up with the timeline, you will notice that this doctor said it was fine to go on my cruise first!

By the way, for the first time in my life, I found out the difference between minor surgery and major surgery. It is minor surgery when it's someone else's. It's major surgery when it's mine! I talked the doctor into releasing me the day after surgery, and I took a few days off. During that time, I wrote a sermon about what I was experiencing, so that I could answer for my congregation the question that I had grappled with: What is a Christian supposed to do when he hears that he has cancer?

I went back to the doctor's office nine days later expecting to hear that everything was just fine because I was sure they had been able to remove all the cancer. However, the doctor said, "We got almost all of it, but according to the pathology report from the lab, you still have some cancer. Hopefully, it will die by itself, which is usually what happens." Now, more than five years later, I am happy to tell you that I am free of cancer, but I am a different man. Facing cancer changes everything.

Cancer Changes Your Attitude

When you hear the word *cancer* from your doctor, your world is changed. How do you respond? What do you do? The first thing I thought was, "I have a choice." I had two options: become really depressed—and I've seen people do that, to the point of devastation—or resolve to praise God no matter what. All of my soul-searching brought me to this one simple answer: "*Bless the Lord, O my soul: and all that is within me, bless his holy name!*" If you are thinking that this is not the natural response to terrible news, you are right. It is a supernatural response! God directed me to Psalm 103 to give me comfort and guidance through this storm in my life.

Verse 3 of Psalm 103 says to bless Him "*Who forgiveth all thine iniquities.*" Our sins are erased! That's enough reason by itself to praise the Lord, regardless of life's circumstances.

Then verse 4 says to bless Him "*Who redeemeth thy life from destruction; who crowneth thee with lovingkindness and tender mercies.*" God is so patient and merciful. The Bible says in the book of Lamentations that God's mercies are "*new every morning: great is thy faithfulness*" (Lamentations 3:23).

Psalms 103:5 says of God that it is He "*Who satisfieth thy mouth with good things.*" I thank God for my family, church family, friends, food, finances, and freedom. I thank the Lord that I can have fun and enjoy life in Christ. If salvation weren't enough, He gives us so many good things besides!

First Thessalonians 5:18 is a wonderful verse that everyone should know and practice: "*In everything give thanks: for this is the will of God in Christ Jesus concerning you.*" When I found out that I had cancer, I knew that I was in the perfect will of God and that He had allowed this disease in my life for a reason. I didn't know why. I didn't have to know why. All I have to do in response to whatever happens in my life is to be faithful and "*in everything give thanks.*"

Cancer is not a laughing matter, but we sometimes laugh at it because it's a whole lot better than crying! I've always preached that we are to be joyful not *because of* our circumstances but *in* our circumstances. Notice that I didn't say that I was happy that I had cancer but that I could be thankful and joyful in the midst of it.

I realize that all cancers are not the same and that my odds were a lot better than some, but I've known others with cancer whom you would never see without a smile. My brother-in-law was diagnosed with end-stage pancreatic cancer, but he remained cheerful all the way until he went home to be with the Lord. It takes courage to live that way. Cancer is not fun, but no matter what your situation in life, you will enjoy it a whole lot better if you learn to be thankful and joyful to the Lord and "*forget not all his benefits.*"

Cancer Changes Your Thinking

While I had a lot of extra time to think, I considered my mortality. Most of us expect our tomorrows never to cease. We expect to continue enjoying life.

Just a year before I received the cancer diagnosis, I had transitioned from serving as the senior pastor at my church, a position I had held for thirty-five years, to traveling as a speaker at church meetings and conferences across the country. I already had meetings scheduled for three years into the future. Life rolls along, and we think that nothing is going to happen, but God teaches us to "*number our days*" (Psalm 90:12).

I suddenly realized, "I have cancer in my body. My days are numbered." I don't know what that final number is. But, because of my mortality, my days of serving the Lord are numbered and I need to give Him my best. The thought occurred to me that *if you live for God today, there will be no regrets tomorrow.* I want to make today count because I am only guaranteed this moment.

Pause for a moment and consider people who have had their lives cut short because of some disease or tragedy. I remember a 19-year-old neighbor that died in a car accident and a college roommate who died over the Christmas holidays. My own mother had a brain tumor and died at 52.

My point is we have absolutely no guarantee of tomorrow. Maybe that is why God said in Proverbs 27:1: "*Boast not thyself of to morrow; for thou knowest not what a day may bring forth.*" All of us ought to stop and consider that our immortal souls are cooped up in mortal bodies. Will we have regrets when this life is over? Perhaps you have never had anything like cancer, but we all need to stop and think, "What am I doing with my life?" Determine to make every day count.

Cancer Changes Your Actions

Having cancer makes you think beyond Earth's shores. I have to ask myself, "What have I done with my life thus far? "*For we must all appear before the judgment seat of Christ; that everyone may receive the things done in his body, according to that he hath done, whether it be good or bad*" (2 Corinthians 5:10).

There will be no judgment for sin at the Judgment Seat of Christ since only Christians will be there. But all of our works and motives, good and bad, will be tried by fire as God tells us in 1 Corinthians 3:11–13: "*For other foundation can no man lay than that is laid, which is Jesus Christ. Now if any man build upon this foundation gold, silver, precious stones, wood, hay, stubble; Every man's work shall be made manifest: for the day shall declare it, because it shall be revealed by fire; and the fire shall try every man's work of what sort it is.*" What will be left standing after the fire falls?

Although the sinful things will be burned up, the good will be left behind, and I will be rewarded for them at the Judgment Seat of Christ. I started thinking about what I would see there. What crowns will I have to lay down at His feet? I wondered, "Have I done my best for Jesus? Are there any changes I need to make now?"

It's so easy to get sidetracked with our work and other activities that we think are so important now. Will those things really be important when we stand before the Lord?

Dear reader, thank God for your job and all the other blessings of this life, but don't lose your perspective on eternity. Ask yourself this question: "Why has God put me in my place of business or in my community?" Are you consistently talking to people about the Lord? Are you doing what God has put you here to do? This life will be over soon. "*And that, knowing the time, that now it is high time to awake out of sleep:*

for now is our salvation nearer than when we believed. The night is far spent, the day is at hand: let us therefore cast off the works of darkness, and let us put on the armour of light. Let us walk honestly, as in the day; not in rioting and drunkenness, not in chambering and wantonness, not in strife and envying. But put ye on the Lord Jesus Christ, and make not provision for the flesh, to fulfil the lusts thereof" (Romans 13:11–14). As for me, I am resolved to do a better job for my Lord, my family, and my church. How about you?

Cancer Changes Your Focus

When I was going through my trial, I was reminded that I am never to ask *why* when going through physical or spiritual suffering but rather *what is it that I am supposed to learn from this?* One thing God showed me is that I receive comfort from God so that I can, perhaps, give comfort to others. "*Blessed be God, even the Father of our Lord Jesus Christ, the Father of mercies, and the God of all comfort; Who comforteth us in all our tribulation, that we may be able to comfort them which are in any trouble, by the comfort wherewith we ourselves are comforted of God*" (2 Corinthians 1:3–4).

During my time of recovery, I saved some emails that I received from a church member who has leukemia. I thought, "He has been through this—and worse." I've watched him through the years continually living for God with a smile on his face, and I wondered, "Will I be able to do that?"

I remember speaking with him and trying to put into words what I was feeling. He said, "I know. You just long for the day when you will feel normal again." It helped me just to know that someone else understood.

When you go through a little suffering, it causes you to understand better the sufferings that so many others go through. It helps you take the focus off yourself and place it on others. You don't always know what to do for those who are suffering and needy, but do what you can.

For several years, my wife Mary had Meniere's disease, which skewed her equilibrium, making her violently sick because she felt as though the room were spinning. While Mary was sick, people often asked sincerely if there was anything they could do to help. I had asked others the same thing many times myself. I was grateful for their kind words, and I knew I could count on them. Sometimes that's all you can do.

There was one particular lady in our church who didn't ask what she could do. Instead she said, "I'll be bringing a meal tonight." More than once she said, "I'm going to come over tomorrow to clean your bathrooms for you." She insisted on shopping or vacuuming or anything she thought might be neglected since Mary couldn't do it. I tried to tell her not to bother, but she came anyway. I learned from her that when you see someone who has a need, you just fill it.

We all need to adopt the motto of the songwriter who penned, "Help me in all the work I do, to ever be sincere and true and know that all I'd do for You, must needs be done for others. Others, Lord. Yes others, let this my motto be. Help me to live for others, that I may live like Thee."

God Never Changes

God is always good regardless of the outcome. I came to that conclusion regarding my cancer. Whether I die of cancer, live with cancer, or am cured of cancer, He is still good, and that will never change!

I experienced God's goodness years ago when my daughter-in-law, Becky, was in the hospital because of a terrible car accident in which she was thrown from her minivan. The doctors did not expect her to live, but God gradually healed her completely, a miracle for which we praise the Lord. During that time, I must have listened a hundred times to a song that she had written and recorded entitled "God is Good" (© Becky Calvert 1992). Here's how it goes:

> God is good; God is good. And He doeth all things well.
> All His efforts meet success. God is good. God is good!

Who am I to question the judgments that He makes?
God is good—this I know. God is good.

When life is a struggle and I feel alone,
When sadness steals my song, God is good.
When surprises come at me, He is not surprised.
For He planned it, He is God, and He is good.

If life smiles on me today or if it frowns,
If the sun comes up or doesn't, God is good.
In a million years from now I'll not remember those.
But I will remember that my God is good!

Praise the Lord! God is always good regardless of my circumstances. Whether or not I am cured of cancer has nothing at all to do with God's goodness.

You may think that a simple lesson, but the idea that God is good is the very thing that Charles Darwin scorned when his son died at a young age. Darwin got angry, threw his fist up at God, and turned his whole life against Him.

If the worst I ever have to deal with is that I will die and go to Heaven where there is no more sin, no more sickness, no more heartache, and no more taxes, a place where I will live with my Savior forever, I have nothing to complain about! Wow, Heaven is a wonderful place! So, if you ever find out that you have any serious physical problem just remember:

Resolve to praise God;
Realize your mortality;
Raise up a good legacy;
Relieve others in need; and, above all,
Remember God is good—regardless!

It would be good to remember these things even if you aren't going through trials right now. All of us will at some time or another go through a trial, but our hardships don't change the fact that God is good. With all that Job went through, he could say, "*The* LORD *gave, and the* LORD *taketh away; blessed be the name of the* LORD" (Job 1:21).

A Necessary First Step

There is an assumption underlying everything that you have just read. That assumption is that at some point in your life you have personally trusted Jesus Christ as your Saviour. I have mentioned salvation through Christ many times throughout this book. Keep in mind that none of us is good enough to go to Heaven on our own merits. The Bible clearly says, "*For by grace are ye saved through faith; and that not of yourselves; it is the gift of God: Not of works, lest any man should boast*" (Ephesians 2:8–9). It's only because of the goodness of God that any of us can go to Heaven.

I'd like to plead with you. If you have not asked Him to be your Saviour, do so today. Just believe He is the Son of God who died to save you and call on Him with a simple prayer such as this: "Dear Lord, I know I am a sinner deserving of Hell. I am totally convinced that You died for me by shedding Your blood and You were resurrected from the dead in order to provide forgiveness for my sins. I now put my complete faith and trust in what You have done for me. Please forgive me of my sins and come into my heart and save me."

Once you know Jesus, you'll understand the peace that I discussed in this chapter, peace to look death in the face and say, "It's okay. God is good."

13

When You Feel Completely Defeated

PSALM 116:1–6

I love the Lord, because he hath heard my voice and my supplications. Because he hath inclined his ear unto me, therefore will I call upon him as long as I live. The sorrows of death compassed me, and the pains of hell gat hold upon me: I found trouble and sorrow. Then called I upon the name of the Lord; O Lord, I beseech thee, deliver my soul. Gracious is the Lord, and righteous; yea, our God is merciful. The Lord preserveth the simple: I was brought low, and he helped me.

What about you? Do you feel like the psalmist who said, "*I was brought low?*" The devil is in the business of taking people down. He goes into the boxing ring with both gloves on ready to fight. Maybe you weren't ready for that uppercut to the jaw. Maybe you hadn't trained long enough to endure round after round of jabs and hooks. Now you're down. You're lying on the mat, bloody and beaten to a pulp.

You wonder, "What happened? How did I end up down here?" You're still reeling from that final blow, and your mind is too cloudy to know what to do. Every fiber in your pummeled body screams, "Stay down. You've been defeated. There is no use in getting back up." All the while, your opponent dances around in his corner, beating his gloves together as he smugly waits for the referee to declare him the victor.

Well, he hasn't won. Let me stand in your corner and shout, "Get back up! The fight isn't over. The count has just begun. You haven't lost unless you stay on the mat. Get back up!"

Yes, you're down, but you don't have to stay down. Maybe you've taken some blows. Maybe you've even messed things up. No matter how defeated you feel, you're not beaten—not yet. You're only beaten if you stay down.

There's Someone else in your corner too. God watches as you lie there motionless and quiet, but then your eyes open, and His heart stirs. "This is it!" He says with eager anticipation. He has just been waiting for any movement that says, "I'm getting back up." You draw your elbows underneath you and pull up in an attempt to bring yourself to your knees, and His pulse quickens. This is the opportunity God has been waiting for. He keeps His eyes on you, waiting to see what you will do next.

You're weak, but you lift your head and look up. Your eyes search the ring until you find His. The moment you seek Him out, the moment you look into His eyes, He says, "Now I can do what I've been waiting to do. Now I can help."

Everyone Faces Defeat

Defeat and despair go with the territory of being human. We've all been "down on the mat." This book has discussed the punches that we all take from time to time. Some of them are unexpected wallops. Others are self-inflicted blows. They all have one thing in common: the devil intends each one of them to be the knockout that declares him the winner.

Relational problems, personal rejection, disappointments, hardship, besetting sins, uncontrolled passions, illness—they all hurt, and each blow can make us feel that we've been defeated. Let me ask you a question, "Does feeling defeated make you defeated?"

This feeling, as all the other feelings we have discussed, is a product of your mindset. Feelings are simply a physical manifestation (adrenaline being released into the body is one example) produced by your brain's response to the information programmed into its subconscious as it is influenced by circumstances. They are not always based on truth, and they are subject to many different factors, making them changeable and, therefore, unreliable. It is very unwise to follow something as volatile as feelings.

The only way you are going to change your feelings is to change the information you are feeding your brain. You need to become a fighter. One characteristic fighters have in common is that they are fighters—they have a mental toughness that keeps them enduring through pain and suffering. Their bodies receive all kinds of information that tell them to give up, but they have fortitude programmed into their minds that overrides the physical agony they experience every time they step into the ring.

One such fighter was James Braddock, who established his boxing career by taking down one opponent after the other with his strong right hand, knocking out many of them in the early rounds of the fight. His first big setback came on July 19, 1929, when he entered the ring with Tommy Loughran for the light heavyweight championship. Loughran was able to avoid Braddock's strong right all night, and Braddock lost the fifteen-round match to a decision.

The right jab that devastated his career was followed by a left hook two months later—the Great Depression. Braddock lost everything. He kept fighting to keep food on the table, but he lost sixteen out of twenty-two fights, and then came the final crushing blow, he shattered his once-powerful right hand. He was defeated.

But Braddock was a fighter, and fighters fight. He fought through injuries. He fought through poverty and hunger. He fought through humiliation. He fought through regrets. And he won. After a long absence from boxing, Braddock picked up his gloves again and clawed his way back to the top. He entered the ring on June 13, 1935, in Madison Square Garden as a ten-to-one underdog—a washed-up has-been—against one of the hardest hitters of all time, Max Baer. Braddock beat all odds when he won the fifteen-round decision to become the heavyweight champion of the world.

Friend, right now you're writing your own story. Is it going to be a story of defeat or one of triumph? It is up to you. Okay, you have taken some hard punches. Yes, you've been knocked down, but let me remind you of something: Getting knocked down is one thing, but getting knocked out is another. Flunking a test is one thing, but flunking a grade is something else. Debating with your spouse is one thing, but divorcing is quite another. Throwing a fit is one thing, but throwing in the towel is another.

Why is it that some people get knocked down and stay down, while others get up, and they're better for having been flat on their faces? Half the battle is knowing that you can get up. And you can. Determine now that your story will be one of success, not defeat.

When I Am Weak, Then Am I Strong

Paul said, "*We are troubled on every side, yet not distressed; we are perplexed, but not in despair; Persecuted, but not forsaken; cast down, but not destroyed*" (2 Corinthians 4:8–9).

Paul, how is it possible to have such a testimony? How is it possible to find the strength to drag yourself off the mat when you are so battered and bruised?

Paul answers, *"for when I am weak, then am I strong"* (2 Corinthians 12:10). How does that make any kind of sense? How does strength result from weakness, as this verse would indicate?

God is looking for the opportunity to show Himself strong. He has to find someone who is weak so that He can be strong through that man. He needs someone who is willing to yield to Him, not someone who is trying to be strong of His own volition. He just needs someone who will look up and acknowledge, "I can't do this, God. I am too weak. I need You to do it through me." That's God's cue to lift up the fallen, to give strength to the weary.

Of the faithful in Hebrews 11, it was said that *"out of weakness* [they] *were made strong, waxed valiant in fight, turned to flight the armies of the aliens"* (Hebrews 11:34). How were they able to fight so valiantly? Through their weakness, they relied on God to do what they could not do.

The strong man says, "I can do this if I try hard." The weak man says, "I can do nothing on my own." He looks to God for His strength and power.

Look to Him

When you are face down on the mat, look up. That's what the psalmist did when he was experiencing trouble and sorrow. In verse 4 of the text, he said, *"Then called I upon the name of the LORD; O LORD, I beseech thee, deliver my soul."* What do we do when problems come? We get on the phone and call our friends. "Do you know what happened? I can't believe they did this to me! This just isn't right!" We should learn to do what the psalmist did and go to God with our problems.

Taking your problems to God doesn't mean leaving them with Him and forgetting them. It means that you leave the *burden* of them with Him, and then do your part to resolve them. If you have gotten yourself into difficulties, try to work out the problems with God's help. If your problem is beyond your control, just leave it with God and say, "Lord, I'm going to trust you to resolve this." Go to God in prayer. Let that be the first thing you do.

The psalmist turned to God in prayer because he knew the Lord's character. *"Gracious is the LORD, and righteous; yea, our God is merciful"* (Psalm 116:5). The Bible tells us that God delights in mercy and that His grace is exceeding abundant. If, when trials come, you feel abandoned by God, if you think God does not care, then you do not know His character. Peter says, *"Casting all your care upon him; for he careth for you"* (1 Peter 5:7). Yes, you will experience trouble and heartache, but God invites you to cast it on Him. He truly does care.

God reminded the people of Judah of this very thing. The prophet Azariah went out to meet the people on their way back from battle to bring them the Word of the Lord. God reminded King Asa and his people that when the nation had turned to God in trouble, He had been right there to help them: *"But when they in their trouble did turn unto the LORD God of Israel, and sought him, he was found of them"* (2 Chronicles 15:4). He encouraged Asa that God would do the same for them: *"The LORD is with you, while ye be with him; and if ye seek him, he will be found of you"* (2 Chronicles 15:2). The Lord is eager to help those who are in trouble, if only they will seek His help. That is our God; *"the LORD is merciful and gracious"* (Psalm 103:8). When you are face down on the mat, call out to Him; seek His help, and He will be found.

Earlier in that same chapter, while the psalmist was experiencing trouble and anguish, the Bible says he turned to the Word of God for encouragement, and that is exactly what he received. He said, *"I know, O LORD, that thy judgments are right, and that thou in faithfulness hast afflicted me. Let, I pray thee, thy merciful kindness be for my comfort, according to thy word unto thy servant. Let thy tender mercies come unto me, that I may live: for thy law is my delight"* (Psalm 119:75–77).

The Bible provides healing, cleansing, comfort, and encouragement. It offers help, and it will change you, if you will just obey it. As a pastor, I have dealt with hundreds and hundreds of people, and there's one thing that is always true about anyone who is under a mountain of problems—they have not been having a daily time with God in the Bible. You can mark it down; they've become coldhearted toward God. If you find yourself pulling away from the Holy Bible, if you get to the place where you think, "Hey, I can get along without reading it today," I guarantee you're heading for trouble. That's where the problems that lead us to feel defeated often begin. Get back to where you should have been.

No matter what has knocked you to the mat, the answer, when you feel defeated, is to go to God. First, go to God in prayer. Second, go to the Word of God. Get into the Bible and draw encouragement from it.

Give Him Control

Your life needs order, and the only way to have it is to start right where you are, resolving one problem at a time. It may seem slow, but it's a start. Don't wait any longer. The mountain of problems will not get smaller by itself, but it will grow without much help. Don't get to the place where you feel totally defeated. Resolve by God's grace, "I'm getting back to the Word of God, I'm getting down on my knees, and I'll take one problem at a time to God to work them out." That's the key: taking the problems to God.

Too often we try in our own strength to work out our problems. We try to manipulate our circumstances. We try to change other people. We try to talk our way out. We try to figure out ways to fix problems. We try and try and try. What usually happens is we make things worse. The Bible says, "*Trust in the Lord with all thine heart; and lean not unto thine own understanding. In all thy ways acknowledge him, and he shall direct thy paths*" (Proverbs 3:5–6). That is a very familiar passage, but are you living it out?

When your first impulse is to say, "Well, I am going to straighten my wife out," stop and ask, "Lord, is that what You want me to do?" When you prepare a speech that is going to change your teenager's rebellious heart, ask, "Lord, is that what I should say? Or should I say anything at all?" Are you leaning on your own understanding, or are you giving God a chance to work?

You and I need to realize how small and finite we really are. We need to understand that we don't understand everything. We need to realize that we do not have the power to change people and circumstances. Only God can do those things. We need to give our problems to the one who can see the beginning from the end, and watch what He can do. *"As for God, his way is perfect: the word of the LORD is tried: he is a buckler to all those that trust in him. For who is God save the LORD? or who is a rock save our God? It is God that girdeth me with strength, and maketh my way perfect"* (Psalm 18:30–32).

There are two key things here. The Bible says, *"As for God, his way is perfect...."* If that's true, then I am to follow the Lord. I am to let God do His work in my life because His way is perfect; He makes no mistakes. Then, according to the Bible, if I submit myself to the Lord, He *"maketh my way perfect."* First I acknowledge Him; then He directs my steps.

Get Back Up

There is one more important principle I want you to notice: failure is not final with God. Job experienced failures, David experienced failures, Paul experienced failures, Peter experienced failures. I could add my name to this list and so could you. All these people give testimony to the fact that God lifts up the fallen.

Proverbs 24:16 says, *"A just man falleth seven times, and riseth up again."* You've been knocked down, but you don't have to stay down in defeat. The answer is not within you; the answer is with God. He is in your corner waiting for you to lift your head up from the mat and call out, "God, help me." That's when He rushes into the ring and picks you up in His strong arms to put you back on your feet. You only need enough strength to keep looking up.

People flocked to watch Joe Grim fight. With each successive fight he gained a greater following, because he was a champion, right? Wrong. Joe Grim really couldn't fight his way out of a paper bag, but people would come to watch his fights because the man could take a horrific hammering and stay in the fight. At the end of every beating, Joe would hold onto the ropes and yell to the crowd, "I'm Joe Grim, and no one can knock me out."

That might be a good mindset for all of us to adopt. The devil will throw discouragements, disappointments, and distresses left and right to knock you out. The next time you have taken a beating, grab the ropes and yell at the devil, "I'm _________. God is in my corner, and no one can knock me out!"

Conclusion

One of the great old hymns of the faith is *What a Friend We Have in Jesus* written by J.M. Scriven/C.C. Converse. Even if they are very familiar to you, take a moment to read the wonderful lyrics. They can offer reassurance when you wonder how to deal with how you feel…

> What a friend we have in Jesus, all our sins and griefs to bear!
> What a privilege to carry everything to God in prayer!
> O what peace we often forfeit, O what needless pain we bear,
> All because we do not carry everything to God in prayer.
>
> Have we trials and temptations? Is there trouble anywhere?
> We should never be discouraged; take it to the Lord in prayer.
> Can we find a friend so faithful who will all our sorrows share?
> Jesus knows our every weakness; take it to the Lord in prayer.
>
> Are we weak and heavy laden, cumbered with a load of care?
> Precious Savior, still our refuge, take it to the Lord in prayer.
> Do thy friends despise, forsake thee? Take it to the Lord in prayer!
> In His arms He'll take and shield thee; Thou wilt find a solace there.

Undoubtedly you've noticed that in every chapter my recommendation has been the same: turn to the Scriptures to find what God has said, and accept Jesus Christ as Saviour if you have never entered into that personal relationship. If you are not a part of the family of God, this counsel may have seemed foolish to you. I understand that reaction. In the first chapter of 1 Corinthians, the Apostle Paul spent a good portion of his letter explaining this type of reaction, *"For the preaching of the cross is to them that perish foolishness; but unto us which are saved it is the power of God…For after that in the wisdom of God the world by wisdom knew not God, it pleased God by the foolishness of preaching to save them that believe"* (1 Corinthians 1:18, 21).

God promises peace and joy that is not subject to life's trials. This is a truth that can be understood only when it is experienced because *"…the natural man receiveth not the things of the Spirit of God: for they are foolishness unto him: neither can he know* ***them****, because they are spiritually discerned"* (1 Corinthians 2:14). If you have never been born into the family of God, then please, take that step now.

Something that is harder for me to understand is why people who give testimony of salvation fail to cast their cares and woes upon the Lord. When we cast our burdens upon Him we are not imposing on God; we are being obedient to Him. Having counseled many believers going through the difficulties I have written about, I believe that the only explanation is found in 1 Peter 5:6–7. The apostle instructs when facing the pressures of life, *"Humble yourselves therefore under the mighty hand of God, that he may exalt you in due time: Casting all your care upon him; for he careth for you."*

Do you see it? It is a lack of humility—the presence of pride—that keeps us from casting our cares upon God. The voice of pride says, "I can handle this myself" even as you are faltering under the weight. When a Christian insists on trying to address life's struggles in his or her own strength, or turns to an unsaved psychologist for help, then he or she is living as the unregenerate live. Paul wrote in 1 Corinthians 3:19, *"For the wisdom of this world is foolishness with God. For it is written, He taketh the wise in their own craftiness.*" If the counselor from whom you receive "help" does not give God's counsel then you are trying to trick yourself into feeling better.

By no means am I minimizing the pain and suffering of a person going through one of the situations I have addressed. The physical, emotional, and spiritual suffering of Job and many others in the Bible is real. And your suffering is real. However, in suffering we can experience victory. When we allow God's Spirit to lead our emotions, He will give us a peace that passes all understanding, and His presence will anchor our souls in God's love.

Remember what Paul wrote in 1 Corinthians 10:13, "*There hath no temptation taken you but such as is common to man: but God is faithful, who will not suffer you to be tempted above that ye are able; but will with the temptation also make a way to escape, that ye may be able to bear it.*" That way of escape is to trust in the Lord. "*Wherefore seeing we also are compassed about with so great a cloud of witnesses, let us lay aside every weight, and the sin which doth so easily beset us, and let us run with patience the race that is set before us, Looking unto Jesus the author and finisher of our faith…*" (Hebrews 12:1–2). Returning to the song…

> O what peace we often forfeit, O what needless pain we bear,
> All because we do not carry everything to God in prayer.

Visit us online

striving together.com

wcbc.edu